From Hippie to Happy

by
Daniel A. Nicholson

ALBURY PRESS
Tulsa, Oklahoma

Unless otherwise indicated, all Scripture quotations are taken from the *New American Standard Bible.*
Copyright © 1977 by The Lockman Foundation,
La Habra, California.
Used by permission.

Scripture quotations marked *KJV* are taken from the *King James Version* of the Bible.

From Hippie to Happy
ISBN 0-88144-026-4
Copyright © 1984 by Daniel A. Nicholson
P.O. Box 121
Central City, Pennsylvania 15926

Published by ALBURY PRESS
P.O. Box 55388
Tulsa, Oklahoma 74155

Printed in the United States of America.
All rights reserved under International Copyright Law. Contents and/or cover may not be reproduced in whole or in part in any form without the express written consent of the author.

Dedication

This book is happily and lovingly dedicated to my dad and mother, Roy and Helen Nicholson, to my dear friend, Mr. Charles F. Freeman, Jr., and to the person who encourages me the most, my precious wife, Betsy.

THANKS!

Acknowledgement

There are so many friends and ministries that I have to thank for the publication of this testimony that they are too numerous to list. I trust the Lord that they know who they are and that He will reward them for all their help to me.

I would like to give special thanks to Bill and B.G. Beitler, Dave and Rose Blackwood, and Don and Helen Michels for their financial assistance in the publication of this book.

Also I would like to thank the Buffington Studios of Clarksburg, West Virginia, for their expert photographic work used in this book.

From my heart, thank You, Lord Jesus!

Preface

It has always been my nature that when I come across something good, I want to share it with my friends.

I know that there are many people in the world today who are unhappy for one reason or another.

In my own case, I spent twenty-three years searching for lasting happiness before I finally found it. Now I would like to share this happiness with you.

Please read this book with an open heart. If you will, I promise you one thing: if you are an unhappy person, you can apply the same principles to your life that I have to mine and you will arrive with the same product, everlasting happiness.

Don't stop now, friend. Happy reading!

1

Are you happy? Stop for a few minutes right now and consider that question. What is happiness anyway? Webster defines happiness as good fortune, prosperity, a state of well-being and contentment, joy or a pleasurable satisfaction.

Someone once said that happiness isn't expensive, but the world is spending millions for an imitation of it. As an American, I "hold these truths to be self-evident, that all men are created equal, that they are endowed by their Creator with certain unalienable rights, that among these are Life, Liberty and the pursuit of Happiness." In the following chapters I would like to share with you my pursuit of happiness.

I was born on May 27, 1952, in Clarksburg, West Virginia. I grew up with my sister and parents in a small four-room house, where my parents still reside, in a small town named Salem, West Virginia. In a small town like Salem, which has a population of about 2,500, just about everybody knows or is related in some way to everybody else. My dad has worked hard all of his life and has always had the philosophy, "If you don't have the money to pay for it, then don't buy it." Now this might not be the American way, but I have always been proud of my dad for never being indebted to another man. I remember working many hot summer days in the hay fields for 50¢ an hour, or mowing lawns for people while maintaining a paper route. My dad thought that I should learn at an early age about the value of money and the responsibility that went along with it. I learned that money could buy a lot of things, but *things* don't necessarily make a person happy.

My childhood was one of innocence with 5-cent popsicles and no facts of life. What I did know, I learned through hearsay from the older boys, and I didn't know what to believe. I was taken to church from the time I was an infant and had accepted it as a place where I was supposed to go once a week. I was taught to believe in God, and yet I didn't know what I believed about Him. As young students in Sunday School, we all memorized the Ten Commandments, the Twenty-Third Psalm, and the Lord's Prayer. My dear mother insisted that I learn and live by the Golden Rule: "Do unto others as you would have them do unto you." I always remembered that one because it seemed to be the most logical of them all. In all the time that I went to church as a young boy, I don't recall hearing anyone ever say, "You must be born again."

My sister, Pam, who was about three years older than I, was born with a hole in her heart. In view of her condition, the doctors informed my parents that she would probably live no longer than six years. Because of this handicap, my sister was never able to attend public school. Instead, our mother taught her at home. She was considered by many to be semi-retarded, but at home she was brilliant and quick to learn. One of the things that I can remember most vividly about my sister was that she was very high-spirited. She did many things on the spur of the moment. However, I considered her to be an ideal playmate. All of the neighborhood children enjoyed her antics, but they learned very quickly that Pam said what she felt, and had a bad habit of slapping anyone who didn't agree with her. But we all looked out for her and she enjoyed life simple and easy.

Pam really enjoyed waiting for me to go to bed so she could put on my blue jeans and cowboy holster and strut around the room. Occasionally, she would put on my boxing gloves and chase me down to show me who was the boss. She was very lovable, but quite unpredictable. One moment she would be petting a kitten and the next moment she would be pulling its tail. Sometimes Mother would bake a pie, set it on the counter to cool, and tell Pam to be sure not to pinch the pie crust. My sister would intentionally pinch the pie crust and then go to Mother and confess, "Mom, I pinched your pie crust." She would sometimes pour Mother's perfume down the sink, and then tell on herself.

Pam really liked to wait on Dad hand and foot. She would have him sit in his easy chair while she brought him the evening paper, put his slippers on his feet, and brush his hair while he read. But when Dad would tell her what a good little girl she was, she would drop the hair brush, do an abrupt about face, and stamp off into another room.

I remember that on one occasion our family went grocery shopping and we took my grandmother along with us. While our parents were in the grocery store, Pam and I stayed in the car with Grandmother to watch over us. We were getting rowdy while playing in the back seat and Grandmother looked for a way to settle us down. Spotting a policeman standing on the corner, she told us that if we didn't settle down immediately she would call for the police officer to come take us off to jail. We thought about what she said for a couple of minutes. I was willing to sit still and be quiet, but Pam decided that she would turn the tables on Grandmother. She rolled down the car window, stuck her little head outside and began to scream at the top of her lungs, "Help! Murder! Police! Help! Murder! Police!" Needless to say, there was never a dull moment with Pam around.

In September 1958, I was enrolled in the first grade. I was excited about beginning this new experience in my life, yet I was a little shy because I wasn't accustomed to being around so many people at one time. All of the children seemed to be friendly and I began to really enjoy going to school. One thing I do recall was being paddled by my teacher quite frequently, although memory fails me as to the reason why. My sister didn't like the idea of my going to school very much because it meant that she would be left at home all day long with Mother and nobody to play with. When I did return home from school, Pam would hide from me. I could always tell when she was hiding from me because she would just stand still with her eyes closed. She thought that because she couldn't see me, I couldn't see her.

At the end of my second year of school, it became apparent that Pam's heart condition was growing worse. On the evening of July 4, 1960, it seemed that everything was going wrong. Pam became very ill and Mother decided to call an ambulance to take her to the emergency room of the local hospital. I could sense the seriousness of the situation as we waited for the ambulance to arrive. To make things even worse, it sounded like the whole neighborhood was setting off fireworks to celebrate the Fourth of July. Suddenly there was an unusually loud explosion that came from our basement. Dad ran downstairs to find out what had happened and discovered that the hot water tank had exploded and that water was running all over the basement floor. Pam was crying uncontrollably as Mother held her in her arms and rocked back and forth in the rocking chair, trying to assure her that everything was going to be alright.

In all of the confusion, I had climbed up to where I slept on the top bunk bed where I felt secure for the moment. From out of nowhere, men dressed in white carrying a stretcher came rushing into the room. They loaded my sister onto the stretcher and started out of the room. For just a moment, time seemed to stand still as I looked down from my top bunk into Pam's sinking eyes. I softly said, "Bye bye, Pammy." As she looked up at me, her swollen blue lips moved and I heard her whisper weakly, "Bye bye, Danny." That was to be the last time I would ever see my sister alive.

July 6, 1960, was Pam's eleventh birthday. On July 27, 1960, she died in the hospital. At the age of eight, I really didn't understand death. The only thing that I did understand was that my sister was gone forever and no one could tell me the reason why. No one could answer my questions as to why my sister had to go away or where she had gone. It seemed so unfair to me because Pam was the only sister I had.

I remember how my Sunday School teacher tried to comfort me by telling me that God needed another angel in Heaven, so He had taken my sister. Of course, now I realize that this is a ridiculous statement because people do not become angels. But at that time I believed it to be true because my Sunday School teacher had told me, and I knew that she couldn't lie. This is one reason why today I believe that if a person doesn't know the answer to a question, he should be honest in his answer and admit his lack of knowledge rather than to say something that might mislead someone, especially a child.

My sister's death was a very difficult thing for my parents to accept. A couple of days after the funeral, I remember seeing my dad standing in our living room and looking up at the ceiling and asking God why He had taken his little girl away. I believe this incident caused my dad to become bitter towards God, because he would never attend church services after that.

Our first Christmas without Pam was a very lonely one. Instead of our traditional silken-haired angel that we usually set on top of our Christmas tree, we placed a picture of my sister. Needless to say, this tragedy had changed all of our lives, and I didn't care very much for the change. I was an only child now and had to face all of the pressures in life that goes with that situation.

It seemed that my mother became over-protective of me, while Dad insisted that I become a man. I felt that my dad was rather strict and harsh with me at times, and I began to fear him and tried to stay out of his way rather than love him. My mother would have one opinion about a certain subject and my dad would have a different opinion. These differences of opinion served to set off many family arguments over the period of the next ten years. Happiness seemed to slip away from me during this time.

I grew up in what I would assume to be a typical small-town atmosphere. I was considered by my parents and teachers to be a rather good student, making only A's and B's for the first six years I attended grade school. I also attended Bible School every summer and began to learn about God, the Creator of Heaven and earth and all that is in them. I never did understand how He did it all, but we were not allowed to ask that kind of questions. I remember receiving several lapel pins for faithful attendance at Sunday School. I would wear them very proudly on my jacket every Sunday.

I led a very active life. I played Little League baseball every summer, and my greatest desire was to be able to hit a home run and win a ball game. I was never able to accomplish that milestone in my life. Some of my most cherished times were those spent playing in the woods behind our house. I would run through the forest and play hide-and-seek with my pet dog, Bugle. I named him that because when we would play together and he couldn't find me, he would howl, sounding like the blast from a bugle.

As we would run and romp across the forest floor, I remember thinking, "Surely, if there is a God, He must live here in the forest." It was always so quiet and calm there. The cool, fresh air and the aroma of the trees and leaves always welcomed me as I entered the woods. All of the trees towered over me and served as a shield from the world outside. I enjoyed watching the animals of the forest as they ate, played, and built their homes. When I was old enough to operate a rifle safely, I would spend many hours in the woods hunting wild game. When autumn arrived, the beauty of the crimson-colored leaves seemed to draw me into the woods to play. It seemed that time passed by so slowly.

The highlight of my six years in grade school was the school Boy Patrol trip to Washington, D.C., in April 1964. It was the first time in my life that I had ever ridden on a train. Needless to say, I was very excited. We visited the Smithsonian Institute, the Lincoln and Jefferson Memorials, and climbed to the top of the Washington Monument. It was exciting to tour the White House and to visit Capitol Hill. I remember on the train on the return trip home, the girl sitting in front of me became ill and vomitted all over herself and the passenger beside her. I thought, "What a finale for an exciting trip."

It was the summer of this same year that I made a decision to accept Jesus Christ as my Savior. I had always attended church, but I had never really committed my life to Christ. For some unexplainable reason, I just felt that this was something that I had to do. Although I still had many unanswered questions about my sister's death, I was nevertheless enthusiastic about the decision that I had made. I ran home from the services that evening, all excited to tell my mother all about my experience and new commitment. At first, I really didn't know how to explain what had happened, but finally I just blurted out nervously, "Mom, I got saved tonight!" Naturally my mother was happy for me; however, I made her promise that she wouldn't tell my dad what had happened because I was afraid that he would think that I was a sissy.

In the fall of that same year I enrolled in junior high school. Actually the school, Salem High School, housed grades seven through twelve, so I was thrust into a new environment with children my own age and also young adults. This was the first time in my life that I began to experience peer pressure. I believed that it was very important to become "one of the gang." I met a lot of new people and made new friends, and thought it necessary to become involved in the extracurricular activities of the school. Within the heart of every person is the desire to be accepted by those around him. I joined the school marching band and learned to play the drums, although I never did learn to read music. I tried out for the junior high basketball team and found the competition to be too great. This was discouraging because it seemed that everyone viewed the athletes as special people, and, of course, I wanted to be accepted.

I had begun to grow out of the shyness of my youth and to enjoy being with crowds of people. I became active in our church youth fellowship group. The year seemed to pass by quickly as we were involved in hay rides, hot dog sales and sled riding parties. By the time September had rolled around, we were all excited about the upcoming baptismal service that was to be held on the banks of a nearby river. I had no idea what water baptism actually meant. I just decided that I was going to let the preacher baptize me because most of my friends in the youth group were being baptized. I waded into the waist-deep water with the preacher and he began to talk to me about what we were doing. Then he said, "I baptize you in the name of the Father, and of the Son, and of the Holy Ghost." Then he dunked me into the water and brought me back up again. I remember afterward that I was joking with one of my friends and said, "Now that all of my sins are washed away, that just leaves room for more." As funny as it may have seemed at the time, that is actually what seemed to happen in my life. I became increasingly dissatisfied and unhappy with my life and my surroundings.

The new semester in school was starting and I was anxious to get back. I really enjoyed the bus trips with the school marching band. For the first time in my life I was becoming interested in girls. The school would sponsor dances in the gymnasium, and all of the kids would attend. This is where I met many young girls and learned to dance. All of these extra interests began to show up in my school grades. I had been an excellent student all through grade school, but by the time I was a freshmen in high school, I was going to all of the school dances, playing in the school marching band, playing on the high school baseball team, and making failing grades on my report card. I was looking for happiness in all of these external things, while on the inside I was becoming more and more unhappy, rebellious, and very inquisitive about life.

I felt I needed to be accepted by everyone; therefore, I began to follow every crowd. I was attending church services almost every Sunday, but it was all very meaningless to me. Soon I had begun to sneak a cigarette with the smokers, drink an occasional beer with the drinkers, learn dirty jokes from the jokers, and play it cool with the thinkers. By the time I was 16 years old, I was doing a little bit of everything and a whole lot of nothing. I was really struggling to find true happiness and meaning for my life. One day while I was sitting in study hall, I wrote a poem, which I entitled "The Question." It really seemed to sum up all of my feelings:

The Question

What is life all about?
Does anyone really know?
People yell and shout,
Protesting all their woe.
This world is full of many fears,
Of many hates built through the years,

*Of many people hurting others,
And yet it's said that we're all brothers.
How can I possibly understand
A world so wrapped in hate;
Where everything is a demand,
And no one knows his fate?
I've pondered this question many times
And yet I still fail to see;
How a world so full of growing crimes
Can live in harmony.
My thought has gone to its full length
And yet I still cannot find the strength;
To understand why people do,
Those hurting things to me and you!*

    Little did I know that I would travel thousands of miles, meet thousands of people, suffer many hardships, and watch several years of my life fade away before I finally found the answer to that question.

    That same year in school I read a book entitled *The Secret Life of Walter Mitty*. If you have ever read that particular book then you know that Walter Mitty was quite a daydreamer. He spent the majority of his time daydreaming about being someone (usually heroic) that he wasn't. After reading this book, I began to fall into the same category as Walter, I became a daydreamer. My grades began to suffer more and more. I became disillusioned with the school marching band and decided to just drop out.

    I spent most of my time in class just staring at the wall and daydreaming about being someone I wasn't. I would usually imagine myself as a real hero, always the underdog type, who would rise to great success and acclaim, as a rock star, a great athlete, a movie idol, or just anything that I was not. All of this daydreaming caused me to become very dissatisfied with life in a small town.

    One of my best friends, Eddy, had quit school and enlisted in the United States Marine Corps and I really envied him. Eddy would write to me and tell me all about what it was like to be a soldier. At this time, the war in

Vietnam was in full swing and I began to daydream about becoming a war hero. High school had become really boring to me and I stopped going to church altogether. I thought that all of those people in the church were hypocrites anyway, and I sure didn't want to be just another hypocrite. None of my friends went to church either. We were too busy getting our kicks from drinking beer and moonshine. I got a job working after school at a local supermarket as a stockboy. I stocked shelves, changed prices on products, and swept up the store after hours. I made enough money to keep myself in cigarettes and to buy enough beer for myself and my friends on weekends. But that particular job didn't last too long. I was fired when the store manager caught me in the stock room eating a pepperoni roll that I hadn't paid for. How disgusting!

Eddy's letters were becoming more and more intriguing and I got the idea in my head that I wanted to quit school and enlist in the Marine Corps just as Eddy had done. I found myself between a rock and a hard place though, because my parents would not allow me to quit school and the Marine Corps would not let me enlist because I was only 17 years old at the time. I only had one more semester of school left before graduation and my grades were nothing to be proud of, simply because I didn't care about studying. My daydreams about the future seemed to be more important to me than anything those textbooks had to offer.

Eddy came home on leave in February 1970, and I skipped every day of school that he was home so I could spend the time with him. I listened attentively as he told me what to expect if I enlisted in the Marine Corps. He actually tried to persuade me not to enlist because, as he put it, "Those guys are crazy!" But the more he talked about the service, the more I became intrigued with the idea of enlisting because it presented a real challenge to me.

Eddy and I were as close as brothers. While he was on leave, we spent the time getting in and out of mischief. My parents could see that I was really determined to have my way so they finally agreed to allow me to enlist on what was called the "180-day delay program." This way, I would be 18 years old in May, graduate from high school in June, spend the summer doing whatever I wanted, and leave for Marine Corps boot camp in August 1970. I became excited on the inside as I began to look forward to what my future might hold.

The last semester of high school seemed to drag on and on as I anticipated what kind of summer I was going to have. After twelve years of school, I could not imagine what it was going to be like to graduate. When I think back on graduation now, I am always reminded of an old song entitled, "I Get By With A Little Help from My Friends," because that is exactly how I got by my final examinations — "with a little help from my friends."

On June 12, 1970, there were 32 seniors in the graduating class of Salem High School. I somehow managed to be one of them. After graduation, we departed in different directions to try to fulfill our own goals in life, many of us never to see each other again. My main goal was to drink and dance all summer long until it was time for me to leave for basic training and finally break away from my boring home town.

Well, the best laid plans of mice, men and high school graduates don't always work out, and mine were no exception. One evening, after I had been drinking all day, I met Rusty, one of my best friends, at one of the local bars. Rusty owned and drove one of the fastest cars in town, and I owned a little 100cc motorcycle. Rusty bragged about how fast his car could go and had earned quite a reputation proving it. After he and I had drunk a few beers together, we decided to go for a drive.

I really wanted to drive Rusty's car, and in just a few minutes I had convinced him to trade vehicles with me just long enough to take a short drive alone. Rusty was a very large young man, weighing over 250 pounds, and I thought it was quite a sight as I watched him straddle my little 100cc motorcycle and go buzzing off down the street. As I drove off in the opposite direction in his race car, I began to remember how Rusty had told me that in this car he could start from a dead stop and burn a streak of rubber over 200 feet long on the pavement. I decided that I wanted to find out for myself if that was true.

I slowly turned into one of the town's side streets and came to a stop. I looked around carefully to make sure that there was no other traffic and no children playing in the street as I slipped the gear shift into the neutral position. Then I slowly worked the accelerator toward the floor board. The engine was roaring as I watched the needle on the tachometer begin to climb from 1,000, to 2,000, to 3,000, to 4,000, finally 5,000 rpm's before I pulled the gear shift into low gear. The rear wheels dug in and smoke began to roll as the car seemed to almost lift itself up off of the pavement. I felt as if my heart were beating in my throat. I had no control over myself to stop now as the car began to inch forward.

Both my hands were firmly clutching the steering wheel as the car continued forward, on and on, roaring and spinning down the side street. Finally the wheels found traction and the car leaped forward like a bucking bronco fresh out of the chute. Quickly I removed my foot from the accelerator and smashed the brake pedal to the floor board. I immediately came to a sliding stop. Momentarily all was quiet again.

I slowly turned the car around and drove back to look at the long strip of rubber I had burned across the pavement. I could hardly believe my eyes as I gazed at the seemingly endless strip of tire marks that stretched down the street. I thought to myself that nobody would believe this story. I decided that I would get out of the car and measure this one for myself. But by that time the whole neighborhood was in an uproar and people were coming out of their front doors to see what all the noise was about. Quickly I leaped back into the driver's seat and sped off down the street, but not before someone had written down the license number of the car I was driving.

I met Rusty a little farther down the road and we traded vehicles again. As I rode my motorcycle toward home I began to wonder to myself if I had done the right thing by not telling Rusty what had happened.

When I arrived home I found that Mother and Dad had gone to visit friends and had left a note saying that they would not be back until late that night. I was still pretty high from all the beer I had drunk during the day, so I decided to take a good hot shower and change clothes before I went out to eat supper. I was almost out the door again when I thought I had better call Sheila, my girlfriend, and tell her what had happened earlier and that I would be over to see her later. I hurriedly dialed Sheila's telephone number and found that her line was busy. I waited a few minutes, dialed again, and the line was still busy. I was growing more and more impatient each time I dialed and heard that busy signal until I became enraged and slammed the telephone down. In a fit of anger I smashed my fist through the living room wall and left an enormous hole. I knew instantly that what I had done was wrong, but I was too angry and too drunk to care. I stormed out of the house, mounted my motorcycle like a drunken cowboy and started out for town to continue drinking.

I had just ordered another large draft beer when I noticed a couple of my friends walk through the front door of the Cozy Corner, a local tavern where I had been drinking for the last hour. They looked rather surprised to see me sitting at the bar, and I invited them to join me.

"What are you doing here?" they questioned.

"It's a free country, isn't it?" I replied.

"Don't you know that the city police are looking for you and have a warrant for your arrest?"

"Why? What have I done to merit this honor?" I asked, thinking they were only joking.

Then they began to explain to me that someone had recognized me driving Rusty's car earlier that day and had called the police. They had sworn out a warrant against me for disturbing the peace, reckless driving, and endangering the lives of their children. Not only did this charge involve a fine, but I was going to be charged a dollar for every foot of rubber tire marks that I had left stretched across the pavement of that little side street. The dollar signs flickered before my eyes as I remembered that enormous strip of rubber that I had burned.

Obviously, I sobered up a lot quicker than I had become inebriated, and the wheels in my mind began to turn in search of a way out of this predicament. First I called the Marine Corps recruiter and asked him what could be the earliest possible day that I could leave for basic training. He told me that he could have my tickets within three days. I told him to have them ready for me to pick up and I would leave as soon as they were ready. Then I straightened myself up as much as possible and went to visit the city mayor.

My parents were friends of the mayor and his wife and I had attended high school with their son. I thought maybe we could talk things over and reach some kind of an agreement. I told him that I had been celebrating because I was leaving for Marine Corps boot camp in three days and that I had drunk a little too much and gotten carried away when I borrowed Rusty's car. He was a nice man and together we found out the names of the people who had filed the complaint against me. He said that if I would be willing to apologize to those people that he would take care of the ticket and fine for me. I agreed and soon I was on the road knocking on the doors of the people who had signed the complaint. One by one I was able to persuade them to be merciful and drop the charges against me. They all seemed to understand when I told them that I was leaving in just three days for the Marine Corps to fight for their country. The mayor disposed of the warrant, and within a matter of a couple of hours, I was back at the bar ordering another large draft.

I was still bragging about how I had pulled the wool over all those people's eyes when the bartender asked us to leave so he could close his tavern for the night. While on the way home, I was stopped by the city police for speeding through town on my motorcycle. The officer actually believed me when I told him that my throttle had jammed and I wasn't able to control my speed. He even offered me his screwdriver so I could fix the problem immediately. I returned the screwdriver to him after some quick, convincing mechanic work, and once again I was on the road for home, without a citation. I was still laughing from the evening's frolic when I parked my motorcycle in front of our house. I was somewhat puzzled to see the house lights still on. Mother and Dad were usually in bed asleep hours before I came in.

As I walked through the back door, the look on Dad's face brought to my remembrance the hole I had left in the living room wall a few hours earlier. My dad was not as easily convinced as the mayor and the police officer had been. It was only the efforts of my mother that kept Dad from destroying me on the spot. We finally agreed that this matter could be discussed more civilly after a good night's sleep. But the next morning proved to be worse than the night before. The only thing that finally cleared the air was the realization that I would be leaving for boot camp in just two days. It appeared that my quick thinking had delivered me from the problem at hand but had also shortened my summer vacation considerably and all of the activities that I had so looked forward to.

Mother cooked my favorite meal for me for dinner and I went out to try to crowd a whole summer's worth of partying into one night. The next day I voiced a sad farewell to Mother and Dad as I boarded an airplane for the first time in my life. My stomach seemed to sink as the airplane lifted off the end of the runway. I could see my parents waving at me from the ground. Finally all familiar surroundings vanished below me. I settled back in my seat and began to wonder what life in the Marine Corps was going to be like.

A smile broke across my face as I recalled the night before when five of us had ridden my motorcycle together down main street. I laughed aloud trying to figure out in my mind how we had accomplished that feat. I had finally escaped from that little town and I had great expectations for an exciting future.

2

The airplane seemed to be falling out of the sky as we approached the runway in Savannah, Georgia. I sat straight back and stiffened in my seat as the wheels touched the ground. We taxied safely down the runway toward the airport terminal. A Marine sergeant wearing a dress blue uniform was standing at the door of the terminal. He was holding a little bull dog on a leash and watched us very closely as we walked by him. Suddenly he began to shout at everyone who was a Marine recruit and directed us to board several buses that were waiting in the parking lot.

We arrived by bus at Marine Corps Recruit Depot, Parris Island, South Carolina, shortly after midnight on June 30, 1970. Immediately we were rushed off the buses and ordered to stand at attention on the yellow footprints that were painted across the pavement. The night air seemed to be especially hot and humid. I rolled my eyes around to study the unfamiliar faces, wondering where they all came from. I could almost feel the heat of that sergeant's breath as he barked orders out to us like we were animals. An icy feeling seemed to grip my insides as I looked upward into the vast darkness of the clouded sky and questioned myself, "My God, my God, what have I gotten myself into?"

From that very first night, it all seemed like a living nightmare. For the next ten weeks it seemed that my only motivation was pure fear — fear of saying or doing something displeasing to a superior, fear of being sent back in training and having to repeat the impossible. I found that a lot of things that look impossible can be accomplished when you are frightened enough. There was great physical and mental strain on everybody and some were not able to hold up under such pressure. Every day we were reminded that we were recruits and not yet worthy to be called Marines. Every morning we would march to the chow hall chanting the same song:

Marine. Marine. Marine.
He's born on Parris Island, the land that God forgot.
The sand is eighteen inches deep, the sun is blazing hot.
He wakes up every morning, before the rising sun,
And runs a hundred miles or more before the day is done.
Marine. Marine. Marine.
Now when I get to heaven, Saint Peter I will tell,
"Another Marine reporting, Sir, I spent my time in hell."
And when I look around me, what will I see?
A hundred thousand more Marines, standing next to me!
Marine. Marine. Marine.

On September 14, 1970, I graduated from basic training with only a handful of the original members of Platoon 379. My parents flew down for the graduation ceremony and the next day I was transferred to Marine Corps Base, Camp LeJeune, North Carolina, for Individual Combat Training. As fate would have it, I had to work 20 days of mess duty before I began my combat training. I finished this training on October 30, 1970, and went home on my first leave. I had a pocket full of money and 20 days of freedom.

As soon as I arrived home, I changed clothes, borrowed my dad's car, picked up an old friend, and went to the local tavern at 10:30 a.m. Nothing like getting an early start. I thought I had an image to live up to as a Marine on leave. While I was home I visited all the bars, chased the girls around, got into a couple of fights, and spent all of my money. All too soon it was time for me to return to active duty.

More than anything else in the world I wanted to go to Vietnam and kill somebody because that was what I had been trained to do. My mother said that she had been praying that I would not have to go to war. When my orders arrived, I was directed to report to Marine Corps Recruit Depot, Parris Island, South Carolina, for a 4-week training school in basic personnel administration. I could do two things really well — shoot a rifle and use a typewriter. It appeared that the Marine Corps already had enough riflemen. I actually cursed and swore and cried when I found out that I wasn't going to Vietnam.

After completing the administration school I was allowed to return home again for the Christmas holidays and then report to my first permanent duty station which was the Second Marine Aircraft Wing, Marine Corps Air Station, Cherry Point, North Carolina. On January 9, 1971, I was assigned the duties of Administrative Clerk in Marine Aerial Refueler Transport Squadron 252.

I began to enjoy my new job and it kept me very busy. I always wanted to do a good job and keep my superiors happy. While working as an Administrative Clerk, I learned arrangement of files and directives, and later assumed duties as Correspondence Clerk, Pay Clerk, Leave Clerk, Discharge and Reenlistment Clerk, Service Record Book Clerk, and helped to train new officer personnel, besides making coffee every morning and mopping the floors.

During my first year in that office I received two promotions and always tried to be friendly with the officers and enlisted men. I was in a good position to do favors for people and many of those favors could have gotten me into trouble had I ever been caught. I certainly learned the truth concerning the old proverb, "You scratch my back and I'll scratch yours." Even officers would come to me at opportune times to ask for certain illegal favors, and I would always oblige. Many nights I would work overtime in the office to prepare for an upcoming inspection. I spent most of my free time in the barracks either watching television or playing a game of ping-pong with one of the guys. Sometimes I would lose a whole pay check in a Friday night poker game that lasted until Sunday morning. Occasionally I would go to the bowling alley or visit the theater, but usually I stayed on base because I didn't own a car.

One night I went to the Enlisted Men's Club with some of the guys from the barracks and everybody got drunk. That club turned into a western-style barroom brawl and the military police had a heyday trying to separate everyone. I noticed that it was mostly a racial fight and I never returned to that club after that night. I had no place for prejudice.

The Administrative Officer of our squadron was a major and he was also my Officer in Charge (OIC). He was an honest man and always worked hard for the betterment of his troops. I respected Major Mack and tried very hard to please him with the performance of my duties. He was also a plane commander and was often out flying a mission.

Periodically, if my work was caught up, the major would sign me on as "extra crew" and allow me to fly on some of the squadron missions. Early every Friday morning, one of our KC-130's would depart for California on what was called a "school run." Marines who were stationed at Cherry Point were flown to Marine Corps Air Station, El Toro, California, and left there for special training. The same flight would usually return to Cherry Point late Sunday night with troops who had finished their schooling or who were coming to Cherry Point for some advanced schooling.

Once I went on one of the school runs and spent the weekend in California. I rented a motel room and Friday night I visited all the night clubs I could find. Saturday I rented a car and drove to Hollywood and looked around for movie stars. That night I toured Disneyland. I was excited when I returned to Cherry Point and spent the next week telling the guys in the office all about my trip. I believe that it pleased the major to see me so excited.

The major's wife was a lady from the Philippine Islands. They had two children; Steven, five years old, and baby Christiana. The lady did not have a driver's license, so usually, when the major was flying, he would leave his automobile in my custody and I would run errands for his wife whenever necessary. Sometimes I would take her grocery shopping or to a church off base where she enjoyed playing bingo once a week. Often I would watch their children while the major and his wife, Nancy, were visiting friends. Once little Steven and I worked together to build a tree house in their back yard. I loved their children and it was always a pleasure to be able to do something nice for them. I felt very honored to be accepted as one of their family, although at times I believe it raised some jealousy among the misunderstanding troops back at the office.

The Non-Commissioned Officer in Charge (NCOIC) of the administration office was a gunnery sergeant whom we all respected. Gunny lived in a trailor off base with his two teen-aged boys and young daughter. He and his wife had some marital problems and the result was a separation. I could tell that it was an undue hardship upon Gunny to try to work and raise a family by himself. Occasionally I would go home with Gunny for dinner and spend the evening frolicking with the children. One evening while Gunny was busy preparing the evening meal, there arose a commotion outside in the street beside his trailer. He walked out to see what the excitement was all about and found his little daughter, who had been roller skating on the side street, had been struck by an automobile and instantly killed. This was quite a shock to everyone and I noticed that after this tragedy Gunny began to drink excessively.

At first I really felt sorry for Gunny and I would tag along with him to all of the off-base bars to see that nothing happened to him. By doing so, I became quite familiar with all of the bars in the area, and soon it became a habit for me to find a way off base almost every evening, with or without Gunny. I began to make new friends in these bars. Some of them were military people and some were civilians. Quite a number of these new friends not only liked to drink, but they also liked to get high on smoking marijuana. I had heard a lot about marijuana through the drug abuse lectures in high school and from watching some military films, but I had never personally smoked it before. Soon I learned that many of the guys in the barracks were also getting high by smoking marijuana. All that I had read and seen in the drug abuse films seemed to arouse my curiosity about marijuana, and soon, for the second time in my life, I began to experience extreme peer pressure to join the crowd and get high.

It really meant a lot to me to be accepted by these

people, so it was not long before I found myself smoking marijuana with them and enjoying it very much. It seemed to provide a pressure release valve from all of the everyday hassle that I encountered in life. Pot parties quickly became a nightly occurrence in the barracks. We would lock our doors and tape around the cracks with masking tape to prevent any of the marijuana smoke from seeping into the hallways. Sometimes we would spend all weekend in our rooms smoking pot and drinking wine together. We really got to know a lot about each other this way. I found that quite a number of my new friends had enlisted in the Marine Corps because they were running from something or someone. They had grown up in big cities all over America and some of them had been using drugs most of their lives. Sometimes I would sit for hours spellbound by the stories that they would tell about their lives before coming into the Marine Corps. I usually would feel inferior to these long-time drug users because I had come from such a small town and my life was not very exciting compared to theirs.

Our parties began to involve more than just smoking marijuana and drinking wine. Some of the guys were also taking different kinds of pills to get high. I became curious as to where all of these drugs were coming from. I soon learned that a lot of them were coming in from California on our school runs. Some guys would carry in a whole seabag full of marijuana from California and never be caught. Because I worked in the administration office some of the guys were bending over backwards to keep me supplied with good marijuana in return for a favor of one kind or another.

One night at one of our parties a guy offered me a little orange-colored tablet and told me it was "orange sunshine acid." He told me that it was a "four-way hit." I accepted it and put it in my pocket, telling him that I would take it later. I had never taken or even seen LSD before and had no idea what a four-way hit was, but I didn't want to appear to be a square in front of all my friends. Later I found that a four-way hit meant that you could take a razor blade and cut the tablet into four pieces and get high four different times. But one evening before I had found this out, I got up enough nerve and swallowed the whole tablet at once. It wasn't a very big tablet and I had my doubts as to whether it was even any good at all. But about forty-five minutes later I lost all my doubts and almost lost my mind along with them.

I began to hallucinate and see all kinds of weird things. Fortunately, I made it back to my barracks and a friend saw that I was really in trouble. This friend had had a little experience with these things and he thought he knew just what to do. He put me into his car and drove me off base until he found a quiet place near a little lake. Then he parked his car and just walked me around in the woods all night. He told me to talk to him and tell him everything I was seeing. Then he would talk to me and tell me that everything was alright and that I would be coming down from the drug any time now. I was imagining that the trees were chasing us through the woods and that the moon was laughing at me while all the stars were burning like sparklers in the sky. This experience continued for about eighteen hours and it was a couple of days later before I could actually think straight again.

The "trip" was really indescribable and at times it was scary, but not scary enough to make me want to quit using the drug. I figured that if I had lived through that trip, any others would be a piece of cake. Soon after that first trip I was using LSD again and again and again.

3

Marines are required to requalify annually with firearms. This procedure usually takes a week or two of practice at the rifle range. The week that I shot for requalification my score was recorded as being the third highest score on the rifle range. Because of the upcoming Marine Corps Eastern Division Rifle and Pistol Matches I was considered for transfer to the Second Marine Aircraft Wing Rifle and Pistol Team. After our squadron commanding officer had approved my orders, I was immediately transferred Temporary Additional Duty (TAD) to Marine Weapons Headquarters Squadron 2 to train for the Eastern Division matches. After completing several weeks of training, our team was transferred to Marine Corps Base, Camp LeJeune, North Carolina, to participate in the Eastern Division matches.

While at Camp LeJeune, I successfully completed a prescribed course of training in advanced markmanship coaching techniques and range operating procedures. I was qualified to be a Rifle Marksmanship Instructor. Our team successfully completed the Eastern Division matches with high honors and we returned to Cherry Point victoriously. While I had been away from the office on Temporary Additional Duty, Major Mack had received transfer orders and was busy preparing to move his family overseas.

The rifle range officer had been pleased with my performance and I was excited that he was trying to get me a permanent transfer to the Second Marine Aircraft Wing Rifle and Pistol Team. But immediately our new administrative officer talked with our commanding officer saying that I was a vital member of the administration office, so my transfer was cancelled.

It seemed very apparent to me after the major was transferred that my superiors saw to it that I always had an overload of work to do. The pressure began to get to me. I submitted an Administrative Action Form to Headquarters Marine Corps, Washington, D.C., requesting a transfer overseas, but my request was returned to me denied. I began to complain to my buddies in the barracks about how hard I was having to work at the office. Someone said, "What you need is some speed."

Methamphetamine, or better known to us as "meth tabs," was a highly-favored stimulant among my friends. I decided to give it a try in hopes that it might help make my days at the office a little more exciting. I went to work one day so charged up that my superiors couldn't give me enough work to keep me busy. I was typing, sweeping, mopping and generally working circles around all of the other office personnel. But there comes the time when you run out of speed and then comes the big crash. It was exciting for me and also very enjoyable to speed all week long, but usually I would end up having to sleep all through the weekend just to rest my body enough to do it all over again the next week.

One of my best friends in the barracks, Joe, suggested that we take a vacation and just get away from Cherry Point for a few weeks. Joe had been separated from his wife for over a year and she was living in Columbus, Georgia. He said that it was necessary for him to go to Georgia in order to sign the final divorce papers. Joe also had a brother living in Boston, Massachusetts, whom he wanted to visit.

We discussed where we should go several weeks before we were able to convince our superiors to approve our requests for twenty-five days of leave. After our requests were approved, our decision was to use our leave time to tour the entire East Coast. Joe owned a sporty Corvette convertible and he bought an eight-track tape player with head phones to put in the car so we could listen to rock music as we traveled.

We were really riding in style when we left Cherry Point, North Carolina. We had a large stash of some potent marijuana and enough meth tabs to last us both for a month. The first stop we made was our nation's capitol, Washington, D.C. As we drove along Pennsylvania Avenue, Joe passed me a joint and I inhaled the heavy smoke deep into my lungs. I began to laugh aloud as I remembered the first time I had visited Washington, D.C., with the school Boy Patrol. No particular incident about that trip was really funny. It was just the fact that marijuana always made me laugh at anything. That was one of the reasons why I enjoyed smoking it. The Washington Monument looked especially high to me that day because I was too.

The next stop that we made was Philadelphia, Pennsylvania, the city of "Brotherly Love." Joe said that they should rename it the city of "Bodily Harm." From Philadelphia we drove north into New York City. I had heard so many stories about the city from my friends in the barracks that I was anxious to see what it looked like. As we cruised through the city traffic with the convertible top down, I noticed out of the corner of my eye that a black boy up on a high wall was about to throw a brick down on us. Before I could warn Joe, the brick richocheted off the hood of the car and cracked the windshield on the passenger side. If we had been going any faster, I'm afraid that the brick would have landed on my chest. There was nothing we could do but keep right on moving, and that we did until we reached the home of Joe's brother in Boston.

It turned out that Joe's brother was a "man about town" who lived in the old section of the city. He took us to several of the waterfront taverns where some of the Mafia figures were known to hang out. After a couple of days of partying, we decided to visit Niagara Falls. We drove straight through into Buffalo, New York, and stopped there for a meal. When we arrived at Niagara Falls it was well past sundown, so we got a room at the Ramada Inn close to the falls. We were so charged up on our meth tabs that we couldn't get to sleep, so we spent the remainder of the night talking to each other about everything we could think of. After taking that much speed, I could hardly wait for Joe to quit talking so I could start. From our room we could hear the roaring waters of the falls and we anxiously awaited the sunrise in anticipation of seeing what we were hearing.

Niagara Falls was breathtakingly beautiful. Joe and I spent the next day sightseeing and taking pictures. I noticed that in our conversation the night before the main topic that occupied Joe's mind was getting his final divorce papers signed. When I asked him if he was ready to leave for Columbus, Georgia, I received an enthusiastic yes. We ate a handful of meth tabs for lunch and were soon back on the road headed south. We figured to stop in Columbus just long enough for Joe to sign his divorce papers and from there go on to Miami Beach, Florida. The only times we stopped between Niagara Falls and Columbus, Georgia, was to fill up the car with gasoline.

We arrived in Columbus on a hot and humid afternoon in August. We were tired from all those hours spent on the road and badly in need of a shower. Joe introduced me to his wife, Suzanne, and his two-year-old son, Chans. I seemed to sense immediately that things were not going to work out as we had formerly planned. Suzanne invited us to take a shower, stay for supper and spend the night at her home. Joe accepted the invitation saying that they would see the lawyer and sign their divorce papers the first thing in the morning, and then we would be on our way to Miami Beach.

The next morning Joe informed me that instead of going to the lawyer, he and Suzanne had decided to reconcile. It appeared that everyone was happy with the reconciliation and we spent the next couple of days getting high and visiting the night spots in Columbus.

The next chore we undertook was to rent a large U-Haul truck and pack all of Suzanne's furniture for the trip back to Cherry Point. Once the U-Haul truck was fully loaded, the trip back to Cherry Point took almost two days. When we got back, we spent several days looking around town for a suitable place for them to rent because at that time there was no base housing available. Joe and Suzanne agreed on renting an attractive trailer that was located several miles away from the Marine Corps Air Station. I truly enjoyed visiting Joe and his family regularly, and it was while visiting their home that the desire began to arise in my heart for a home of my own.

I was feeling especially lonely one evening at the barracks, so I asked a friend if he would allow me to use his car to drive to the beach and just look around. He agreed to let me take his car and I was immediately on the road headed for Atlantic Beach. I decided to stop off along the way at a bar in Newport and have a cold beer before going on to the beach.

It had been several months since I had visited the John Bar with Gunny. But I remembered that there were a few nice-looking waitresses working there and I figured that anything would be an improvement over most of the women that I was used to looking at on base. Almost all of the female Marines that I knew could outdrink, outcurse, outfight or outrun me anyway, and that was pretty embarrassing.

That evening I was introduced to an attactive young waitress named Debby, and a new relationship began. That first evening we smoked some marijuana and got high together, and I drove her home after she finished working at the bar. We sat in the car in front of her parents' house and the time drifted away as we talked about foolish things. Debby and I began to spend every evening and weekend together. If I couldn't borrow someone's car to go see her, then she would borrow her brother's car and come pick me up.

An entirely new social life began to unfold before me as I met many of Debby's friends at the bar where she worked. We began to realize that we were both filling an emptiness that was in our lives and we thought that we were finding happiness together. I felt that I was falling in love with Debby, but I wanted to be sure that it was more than just a feeling before I said anything to her about it. We had both been hurt in relationships in the past and I wanted to avoid the possibility of either of us going through that pain again.

One evening in January 1973, Debby and I decided to double date with some friends, Dave and Sandy. We were going to visit one of the beach bars for an evening of dancing and drinking. Dave voluntarily drove his car to the beach that night. We were sitting around our table enveloped by the feverish music of the band when someone entered the tavern to proclaim, "Hey, it's snowing outside!" This was an unusual occurrence for Atlantic Beach, North Carolina, so we all ran outside to observe this unexpected phenomenon. Some of these people were thrilled to see snow for the first time in their lives. The beach was soon blanketed by the swiftly falling snow and the flurries were rapidly changing into a blizzard.

We decided that we had better get back to Cherry Point before we became snow-bound. We were about twenty miles from the Marine Corps Air Station and the roads were already covered with snow. Dave thought that he knew a short-cut back to the base so we decided to take it. He had never driven on icy roads before and the lack of experience was evident as we soon found ourselves in a ditch and unable to get out. As a last resort, we abandoned the car and began to walk down the road.

The blizzard had become so severe that we decided it would be safer if we left the road. We feared being struck by a car that might be unable to see us because of the blinding snow storm. We were all dressed in light clothes, not expecting anything like this, and the air seemed to grow colder and darker with every step we took. Fear gripped our hearts as hand in hand we wandered aimlessly along the beach. We were actually blinded by the snow that clung to our faces, and in my heart I thought, "Oh God, help us!"

Suddenly we literally walked into the side of a house. We found our way around to the front door and began knocking frantically. A young couple opened the door and invited us in from the bitter storm. Little did they know at the time that we would be their house guests for the next two days. The radio news informed us that fifteen inches of snow had fallen that night and it was probably the worst snow storm of the century for that area.

In two days we had eaten everything in the house and had smoked a pound of marijuana that the young couple had on hand. We were now without food and quite concerned about how much longer this situation would last. Sandy suggested that we try walking the few miles back into Atlantic Beach in hopes of finding a grocery store open. I concluded that the journey would be too cold and risky to attempt, but Dave and Sandy grew impatient waiting and began the long walk without us.

About an hour later, Debby and I hesitantly stepped outside to try and follow the trail left by Dave and Sandy. We felt bad about letting them go alone. We had walked less than a mile when fortunately a man driving a four-wheel-drive vehicle stopped and offered us a ride which we gratefully accepted. Upon arriving in Atlantic Beach, we discovered that all of the stores were closed so we set out in search of Dave and Sandy. Debby suggested that we try looking at a nearby trailer park where she and Sandy had some mutual friends. Her assumption was correct and we found lodging for another night at their friend's trailer. Debby was able to telephone her mother from a nearby pay phone and let her know where we were and that we were all safe.

By the next evening the roads were clear enough for Debby's mother to drive down and pick us up. Dave and I were happy to get back to the barracks and find out that we were not in trouble for being absent so long. I felt that the whole situation had served to draw Debby and me a little closer to each other. But within a few weeks, my feelings had proven to be deceiving.

One of Debby's best friends, Linda, had recently moved back to North Carolina from Georgia. They had not seen each other for many months so Debby asked me if it would be alright for her and Linda to have a night out on the town together. I agreed and began to make plans for what I might do that evening without Debby. I had recently purchased my first automobile, a 1966 MG sports car. I decided that we had to have our own car for our dates and for Debby to use to get back and forth to her jobs. Besides working as a waitress at the bar, Debby also worked as a babysitter in a day care center at a local church.

When Saturday night rolled around, Debby went out on the town with Linda, while I spent the night partying with some of my friends from the barracks. My buddies and I took some LSD and spent the entire night driving my car all over town, smoking pot and talking each other's heads off. We arrived back at the barracks around 5:00 a.m. I was still high on LSD and decided to wash all of my dirty clothes just to have something to do. I was rapidly running out of things to do when it occurred to me that Debby's mother was out of town for the weekend and Debby would be home alone. Since it was Sunday morning, I decided that I would do my good deed for the day by going over to Debby's house to cook her breakfast and serve it to her in bed.

I walked into Debby's house unannounced and found Linda in the kitchen making breakfast.

"Where is Debby?" I asked.

"She is still in bed, but I don't think you should bother her," said Linda.

I didn't ask her why, but instead I quietly slipped into Debby's bedroom. To my utter amazement I discovered Debby with a young man still asleep in her bed. I found out later that the young man's name was Carl. To avoid any uncontrolled violence, I simply turned around and walked out of the house. My heart was shattered. I felt numb all over as I drove back to the barracks and tried to think of what I was going to do. Hate, anger, hurt and self-pity began to rise up within me. All of the happiness that I had known with Debby had seemingly vanished before my eyes and I was left empty. I felt that I wanted revenge, but yet I just didn't know what to do.

When I returned to work Monday morning, I explained my whole situation to Gunny. He was very understanding and approved my request for ten day's leave. I thought it might help if I just got away from there for awhile and tried not to think about it. I bought all the drugs that I could afford, packed my little car and left the next morning for West Virginia. I decided that when I got home I was going to show my old friends what it really meant to party. After I had been home for a couple of days I found that most of my old friends had let their hair and beards grow long and had already been using drugs for awhile. I spent the next several days getting high with them and trying to forget Debby. I sold our MG and bought a 1968 Volkswagon Squareback.

The ten days passed quickly and it was time to return to Cherry Point. I felt that the time had served its purpose and that I had gotten over my heartache. I went back to North Carolina with only five months of active duty left to serve on my three-year enlistment in the Marine Corps.

4

"I'll be free in '73" was a familiar slogan that could be heard echoing through every barracks on Cherry Point from Marines who were expecting to be released from active duty that year. Actually we didn't know what freedom really meant, aside from our own narrow definitions. I just wanted to get out of the Marine Corps, let my hair and beard grow, get high every day and spend the rest of my life relaxing on the beach and being a "happy hippie."

I had already gotten a part-time job as a bartender at the tavern where Debby worked as a waitress and I had many friends there. Most of those friends were Marines, like myself, who had only a short time left to serve on active duty. However, some of them were ex-servicemen, or civilians, like Jimbo, the tavern owner's son. We began to stick pretty close together and watch out for one another. In the short time that we had known one another, we had organized our own little clique and called ourselves "The Family." We developed a personalized handshake and each member wore a special leather wrist band. Only selected persons were asked to join our group and non-members would stand by in envy as they observed our loyalty to one another. We shared all of our possessions in common and we saw to it that there was always a large stash of various drugs on hand. Meth tabs were a "family favorite."

One evening at the bar I was really buzzing on some meth tabs when I noticed a really attractive young woman walk onto the dance floor. I admired her dancing ability and soon found the boldness to inquire about her name. "The name is Katina," she said, "but my friends just call me Cat!"

I called her "brown eyes" for obvious reasons and soon I learned that she loved meth tabs too. I immediately turned her on to some "white crosses" and we could have danced all night. Later on in the evening when we had become a little better acquainted, Cat informed me that she was presently living with a guy named Carl. As fate would have it, this was the same Carl that I had found at Debby's house early one Sunday morning. I recounted the whole incident to Cat and asked for her opinion about the situation. "If they want each other so much, I don't think we should stand in their way." she said.

I agreed entirely. This looked like a golden paved avenue of revenge to me. About a week later, I rented a house trailer in New Bern and Cat moved in with me. This move proved to be quite expensive and my part-time bartender job was a real help. I recommended Cat for a job at the bar and my boss agreed to hire her as a go-go dancer. Everything seemed to be working out really smooth between us. I was working on base from 8:00 a.m. to 4:00 p.m. and tending bar from 6:00 p.m. until 2:00 a.m. several nights a week. Cat was also working six nights a week. We were doing a lot of partying besides and I was becoming very dependent upon speed to maintain the demanding schedule I had set for myself. At this point in my life, I felt that I was beginning to experience real happiness.

Then one evening when I was working and Cat wasn't, she borrowed my car to drive to Atlantic Beach to meet with an old friend of hers. Later that evening I became concerned that she had not yet returned. She had promised to return shortly and it wasn't like Cat to break a promise. After a few hours of impatiently waiting, I decided to leave the bar and go to the beach to look for her. Before I got out of the bar, a friend came in who had just been on the beach and informed me that he had witnessed Cat being arrested and my car being impounded. I immediately hitched a ride to the beach and very cautiously entered the Atlantic Beach Police Station to inquire about Katina and the possibility of retrieving my car. After much deliberation I was allowed to leave the station with my car. But the only information I could get concerning Cat was that she had been taken to the county jail and I would have to wait until Sunday visiting hours to see her.

That night I returned to a lonely trailer in complete bewilderment as to why Cat was in jail. It seemed like eternity waiting for Sunday to arrive and our first visit was an awkward one. I had never been in a jail before and the Beaufort County Jail had very little to offer as far as I could tell. My heart really reached out for Cat when I first saw her standing alone in that dingy little cell. It was at that moment that I believed I had fallen in love with her.

The first visit was a short one and it wasn't until later on in a letter that Cat explained to me why she had been arrested. The charges against her were quite serious. While she lived with Carl, they had been involved in selling drugs. They were a little careless in one of their deals and had fallen into a trap. A federal agent had purchased a quantity of marijuana from them and therefore the case against them was pretty solid.

Every Sunday afternoon for the next few weeks I would visit Cat and take her a good hot meal. Occasionally, I would enter the jail with a hit of LSD hidden inside my mouth. When visiting time was over we would kiss good-by and I would slip the LSD into her mouth so she could get high. It was the only form of entertainment that I had to offer her and she appreciated it. Sometimes on Sunday afternoon our conversations would be strangely interrupted by a group of young people standing outside in the courtyard singing, "What a Friend We Have in Jesus." Cat would listen closely and say that she really liked that song but I really never gave it any thought then.

After a few weeks had passed, Cat's parents decided to put up a property bond in order for her to be released into their custody while awaiting trial. Cat didn't like this arrangement because it meant that if she decided to run away, her parents could lose all of their property. But this was her only possible way of escaping that lonely jail cell, so she consented to the agreement.

Our reunion was on Easter Sunday and I was invited to her parents' home for Easter dinner. It was wonderful to be together again without any bars between us. The sun shined brightly against the deep blue sky and I noticed the beautiful fluffy, white clouds lazily drifting along as we all played lawn croquet together that afternoon. Later on that day, Cat and I hid Easter eggs all over the lawn for the children who were visiting. After the evening meal, it came time to sit down and seriously discuss the issue at hand.

Cat was now living at home, under her parents' custody, but she argued with them that it would be best for all concerned if she were allowed to move back into my trailer. Of course I wanted her to move back in with me, but I was in a very awkward position to say anything. I sat silently by and just listened as the conversation intensified. Although her mother cried and her father disagreed, Cat was steadfast in her convictions and they finally gave in to her request. The only stipulations were that she keep in touch with them and with their lawyer. It felt so good to have her by my side again as together we drove down the highway toward our trailer. That night, we snuggled warmly together on our living room couch and watched "The Wizard Of Oz" on television.

Carl heard the news about Cat's arrest and decided to run away before the police had a chance to arrest him too. He went A.W.O.L., (absent without leave), from the Marine Corps and left the state. Shortly thereafter, we received a report that he had been killed in a barroom fight in Kentucky. I figured that he had it coming, but the report really seemed to disturb Cat. This meant that the whole drug case now rested in her lap. I knew she would have left the state too if she hadn't been under that property bond.

Cat was really under a lot of pressure now and became increasingly restless as the trial drew near. She even became concerned about living with me now because we had been informed by her lawyer that the police had placed us both under surveillance. Then about 3 o'clock one morning, Cat raised up in bed and said, "I'm leaving!" She had some friends in a motorcycle gang who lived in a town about a hundred and twenty miles away. She made up her mind that she was going to stay with them until the trial and there was no changing her decision. She rolled out of bed, packed a few things in a bag and went out the door with the intention of hitch-hiking a ride there immediately.

I ran out the door behind her pulling my clothes on and trying to convince her to let me drive her. She finally consented to allow me to take her as far as the interstate highway. When we arrived at the highway, Cat was fast asleep and I used the opportunity to take her the rest of the way to her destination. After we arrived in Raleigh, I had to call my squadron office and come across with a pretty good lie as to why I couldn't come to work that morning.

Upon returning to the trailer that afternoon, I sensed a very real feeling of loneliness. I had grown quite fond of Cat and it was hard for me to get used to not having her around. As the days went by, friends would come over to get high and attempt to cheer me up. But their good intentions only caused me to miss Cat all the more. A couple of weeks had passed by and I had received no word from her. Then one afternoon she just walked in. I was thrilled to have her home again but she was tired and seemed to want very little to do with me.

A few days later Cat went to court. I didn't go to the trial and afterwards she wouldn't discuss the results with me. She was convicted and sentenced but, to everyone's surprise, the sentence was suspended and Cat was placed on probation. The police really had her under their thumb. It was rumored that Cat had made an agreement with the police to be an informer about the local drug scene in exchange for keeping her out of prison. When that rumor got back to "The Family," it was decided that it wouldn't be safe to have Cat around anymore. Before I ever had the opportunity to explain this decision to Cat, she came back to the trailer and packed all of her belongings and moved out. With her, she took a little piece of my heart. I couldn't stand to live in that trailer without her, so I moved back into a room in the barracks. I only had a couple of months left to serve on active duty then.

5

Some of the guys in "The Family" had rented a five-bedroom house not far from the bar where I was working. They invited me to move in with them and I accepted. It was good to get out of that lonely room in the barracks and into a home atmosphere. From then on life became a continuous party. I was due to be released from active duty on June 29, 1973, and that month had finally rolled around. Like every other short-timer, I was marking off the days on my calendar. Only fifteen more days and I would be free. My ambitions were to just get out of the service, let my hair and beard grow and hang around the beach all summer being a "happy hippie."

One Thursday afternoon at 4:30 p.m. I was arriving home from the base. I was going to change clothes, grab a sandwich and then head for the bar. I was supposed to start tending bar at 6:00 p.m. As I turned into the driveway I noticed two strangers sitting on our front porch. I also noticed that they were passing a joint between them. This wasn't a very wise thing to be doing because our landlord lived next door and he was a local police officer.

I walked up to the porch and introduced myself and asked who they were and what they were doing there. They introduced themselves as John and Brad and said they were looking for Doc. Doc was one of "The Family" who also lived at our house. I informed John and Brad about our landlord then invited them inside to talk. Doc wouldn't be home for awhile, but they insisted upon waiting for him. The atmosphere became a little more relaxed as we shared a joint together and began to talk more freely about ourselves. It was apparent that I had won their confidence and they began to tell me why they wanted to see Doc. They had come down from Indiana to check out the drug market in our area and they intended to approach Doc about moving large quantities of drugs for them. There was much money to be made in these deals if we were willing to take the risk.

Doc had not yet arrived when I was leaving to go to the bar. John and Brad decided to leave a message and a pound of high grade marijuana at the house for Doc and talk with him later. I stashed the marijuana in the house and went on to the bar in hopes of having an exciting evening. Doc was at the bar when I arrived and we sat down to a cold beer as I informed him of my encounter with John and Brad. I told him where the stash was hidden and he headed for home as I mounted my position behind the bar.

Later that evening, a friend came into the bar and told me that our house had been raided and Doc had been taken to jail. This was something "The Family" never dreamed would happen to us. We were always very cautious in all of our dealings. The whole situation began to feel like death creeping in around us. I decided to call the jail and see if Doc could be bailed out. They said he could, and soon "The Family" got enough money together to pay Doc's bond. I left the bar with two other members of "The Family" and headed for the jailhouse to get our brother out. I instructed the others to take the money in and get Doc out while I stayed hid in the car. I figured that if I went in, the police might decide to keep me there. Within twenty minutes we were speeding down the highway and Doc was telling us how the raid had taken place.

Our landlord had seen Brad and John on our front porch passing a joint between them, so he called the sheriff and the raid was planned. A roadblock had been set up just down the road from our house and John and Brad were stopped only moments after they left our house. They were arrested for possession of marijuana and taken to jail. In the meantime, I had taken another route to the bar in order to get to work on time. Doc was home alone when the police came crashing in. I had informed Doc at the bar earlier where the stash was hidden. Under much pressure and in hopes of getting a lighter sentence, Doc decided to tell the police where the marijuana could be found.

As Doc continued to explain everything, I heard a siren and noticed red and blue flashing lights quickly approaching from behind. It was a police car and we were being pulled over. My heart sank as the officer shined his flashlight into the back seat of our car and directly into my face. He motioned for me to get out of the car and demanded to see my identification. After seeing my identification, he handed me a warrant for my arrest and read me my rights. Within minutes I was stepping out of the police car and into the jailhouse.

As I heard the cold steel bars clank shut behind me, an icy feeling of fear began to grip my heart. Now what was I going to do? I demanded my rights. Didn't I get a phone call or something? No one answered as I stood enveloped in the darkness of that cell. I felt so very helpless.

Many thoughts rushed through my mind, but one was predominate. I had served three years of honorable service in the United States Marine Corps and now within fifteen days of my release from active duty, my honorable discharge was in jeopardy. I found an empty bed in the corner of the cell and sat down to ponder my situation. No doubt about it, I needed a miracle! My thoughts turned to God and I found myself trying to talk to Him. This was not unusual for me. Many times in the past I had found myself in tight situations and I would make "deals" with God. Each time was a little more difficult because I would remember that I had never kept my end of any of those "deals."

"Dear God," I said somewhat embarrassed. "Here I am in another mess and I sure could use Your help. God, I promise if You just get me out of this one, I'll straighten up for sure!"

A moment of silence passed and I felt a little more peaceful. But then the nagging thoughts began to hit me. What kind of a hypocrite are you anyway? You quit going to church because of hypocrites and now look at you trying to talk to God after all that you've done. What nerve! Besides, God doesn't care about you anyway or He wouldn't have let this happen to you in the first place. That's right, I thought, as I drifted off to sleep wondering why God had let this happen to me.

I woke up the next morning and found myself in a cell with ten other guys among whom were Brad and John. I skipped the breakfast of green eggs and burnt toast. Brad, John and I sat together and talked for a couple of hours about our predicament. In the conversation, Brad mentioned that they had rented a motel room a few miles away and had a large stash of drugs there. They needed to get word to someone on the outside to go to that motel room and remove their possessions before room service discovered their stash. There was enough in that room to send them up the river.

Later on in the morning, a police officer came to the cell and asked me to follow him out of the cell and into the Deputy Sheriff's office. To my surprise "The Family" had gotten enough money together to pay my bail and Doc had come down to take me home. But before we were allowed to leave, the Deputy Sheriff thoroughly questioned Doc and me about our involvement with Brad and John. The police had been watching them for a long time and they needed some solid evidence against them to make this stick. Doc and I refused to give them any information even after we were threatened and bribed.

It was a real relief to walk out of that jail, but what was I going to tell my superiors back at the base? I figured that I would be in the brig before nightfall. That afternoon I went into my office prepared to face the music. To my utter amazement I was received as if nothing had ever happened. After questioning some reliable friends, I got to the bottom of it all. Apparently all the little "favors" I had dished out over the past several months had worked out for me.

A certain lieutenant had heard all about the bust from some friends of mine at the bar. This lieutenant and I used to smoke pot and drink wine together and I had pulled a few strings in his favor in the past. So he told a few lies and covered for me at the office and I was home free. I could hardly believe my ears. I was really off the hook! I had to appear in court on July 12, but my discharge date was June 29, so my honorable discharge was still in the bag, and that was a relief.

The next day I sat down with Doc and shared with him everything that Brad and John had told me about their stash at the motel room. We thought long and finally reached a decision. There were warrants out for the arrest of every "Family" member who lived in the house. John and Brad had made some stupid mistakes and "The Family" was suffering the consequences. Doc and I decided that if we could get the rest of "The Family" off the hook by telling the Sheriff that we knew about John and Brad, then we would do it.

We went to the Deputy Sheriff with that proposition and he agreed to make it easy on us. The rest of "The Family" would have to post bond, but our cooperation promised to keep us out of prison. Doc and I were required to ride to the motel with the Deputy Sheriff. It was a long, uneasy ride. When we arrived the motel owner unlocked the door to Brad and John's room. After a little searching, the police found two suitcases with enough evidence to send Brad and John up the river. The only thing left to do was for Doc and me to testify in court.

On June 29, 1973, I was released from active duty with the United States Marine Corps with an honorable discharge and the Marine Corps never found out about my arrest. I called my mother that day and told her I had been discharged and that I was going to stay in North Carolina for awhile before returning home. I told her I wanted to look around for good job opportunities. I didn't have the nerve or the heart to tell her of the trouble I was in. That night I invited a lovely young lady out to dinner to celebrate with me. We had a wonderful meal of steak, lobster and wine. After dinner, I took a hit of LSD and we went to the bar where I worked. "The Family" and all of my friends threw a surprise "Discharge Party" for me at the bar with cake and all of the trimmings. It turned out to be a really wild night.

I continued working at the bar and also had signed up to receive unemployment checks. I figured I would take whatever I could get. Our court date was July 12, and it seemed to come all too quickly. We were all a little nervous about what might happen. That morning in court, there were eighty-four other cases on the docket. Everything from oystering in closed season, to indecent exposure, to possession of heroin. Our case was finally brought before the judge. After a careful review, he determined that because of the seriousness of the charges, the case would be bound over for Superior Court, which would meet in October. In the meantime, none of us was allowed to leave the state of North Carolina. We went home that day wondering how all of this was going to work out.

6

I had made up my mind that I was going to have a happy and exciting summer. I was free from the bondage of the Marine Corps and all the hassle that went with it. No more "Yes Sir, No Sir" for me. I was going to be my own man. I went out and got a job with a construction company and worked for two days, then quit. I did this purposely just to see what it felt like to look at a superior and say, "I quit," and walk off the job without fear of a Court Martial. I did continue working as a bartender though.

There were many benefits to that job which I found very appealing. There were two other bartenders and we worked out a schedule among us that seemed to please everyone. Usually I would work five days a week, starting at 6:00 p.m. and closing the bar around 2:00 a.m. Then, "The Family" would go somewhere and party until sunrise. When the rest of "The Family" was going to work or "crash," I would take a blanket to the beach and lie in the sun until the tide came in and woke me up. I got a great tan that summer. The only problem was I almost drowned twice when the tide came in to wake me.

I would spend the rest of the day loafing around the beach seeing what I could get into. There were always a few ladies running around looking for a good time. I would usually invite one or two to the bar that evening and many times they would be hired as waitresses or dancers. I met bunches of girls in this fashion. The turnover in waitresses and dancers was quite high, so I always kept my eyes open for new prospects.

Sometimes while tending the bar I would watch the front door for new faces coming in. If I saw a girl I didn't recognize or wanted to meet I would motion for her to come to the bar and came across with a line like this: "Because I have picked you from the crowd as the most attractive creature here, you may have your choice of a drink, on the house." Sometimes she might sit at the bar and drink for free until closing time, then go home with me. Sometimes two or three would come home with me and stay and party all night with "The Family." This life style was addictive. The more I did it, the more I wanted to do it.

I was always looking for excitement or a good time. Continually seeking to be happy. I was selling drugs from behind the bar and taking big chances. Finally I quit tending bar and just sold drugs for profit. Sometimes I would walk around with several thousand hits of L.S.D. in my pockets or hidden in my car. Inside I carried a constant fear of being busted, yet I went on.

One time I was sitting in a chair right outside the front door of the bar. It was hot inside so I had taken the chair outside to relax and drink a cold beer. Suddenly I looked up and the parking lot was filling up with police cars and policemen. Then all the policemen came rushing toward me. I was petrified. The bar was being raided and all of those policemen rushed past me and into the bar. I had two ounces of marijuana in my back pockets and my front pockets held several hits of speed. As soon as the last policeman ran past me, I was on my feet and running into the woods behind the bar to empty my pockets. That was only one of many close calls. The bar was always under surveillance.

"The Family" had some pretty good contacts with drug dealers and we were always getting something new to use and sell. We were very cautious about whom we sold to. We knew most of the "narcs" on the beach and avoided them and the places they hung out. Rock concerts were the big thing that summer and we went to every one we could get to. I had quit shaving and my hair was growing pretty long and I felt right at home with all the other freaks at the concerts. We traveled up and down the East Coast that summer to hear all the big names: Alice Cooper, Santana, Tower of Peace, The James Gang, Dr. Hook, Fog Hat, etc. The list was endless.

The entire summer was one big party. Many times we would stay up on speed or acid for several days at a time and then really do some crazy things. One morning after being up on acid for several days, Toby, another ex-Marine, and I were drifting around the beach looking for something to get into. We jumped into my car and took a drive down the beach until we approached a Coast Guard base and decided to have a look around. There was a big ship in the harbor. We parked the car and walked over for a closer look. It seemed to be deserted so we walked over for an even closer look. Immediately we were spotted by the Officer of the Day and asked for identification and our purpose for coming aboard ship. He saw by our I.D. cards that we were ex-Marines and after some small talk, we persuaded him to take us on a tour of the ship. He was friendly and answered all of our stupid questions.

Finally we found ourselves on the top level of the ship looking up to the "Crows Nest." We asked permission to climb up to the "Crows Nest," but the officer said we were not allowed. But we climbed up anyway. He began to warn us to come down immediately, but we refused to listen. Upward we climbed until we were on the highest point on that ship. Wow!! The view was spectacular. The water below us was beautiful and the breeze refreshing. I felt bold.

I began to tempt Toby by saying, "I'll do a swan dive if you will jump." Of course I was only teasing, but the next thing I knew, Toby was in mid-air and quickly descending out of sight. The next thing I saw was a little white splash in the water below. I thought I would die laughing when I looked down to see the expression on the officer's face. He began to blow his little whistle and shout through his bull horn, "Man overboard, man overboard."

Someone else set off some kind of an alarm and a life preserver with a rope attached was thrown out toward Toby. Toby was calmly treading water and motioning for me to come on down. Now I was a man of my word, not to mention being higher than a kite, so, bombs away. I felt like an eagle diving on his prey for about five seconds. Then I was engulfed in the warmth of the water. When I came up I heard more bells and whistles and the officer shouting over his bullhorn, "Two men overboard." Toby and I swam to the dock and climbed out of the water. We could hear the officer in the background screaming something about "crazy Marines" as we made our way to my car. We drove back to the beach for a cold beer to wash down the salt water.

Another time, after partying for days, I was driving down the road with a friend and we had to stop at a railroad crossing while a freight train passed by. While my friend was talking, I had a sudden urge to ride a train. I put my car in neutral and leaped out. I ran alongside the train and managed to climb on as my friend sat in my car looking in amazement. I rode the train into the next town and nearly killed myself when I leaped off. I thumbed a ride to the bar and found my friend and my car waiting.

The parties continued on through the summer, marathon after marathon. It seemed as if our mischief begat more mischief. Rather than having us busted again, our landlord stormed into our house one morning after a three-day marathon party and informed us that we had thirty minutes to evacuate his house. There were bodies laying all over the floor and everyone was wondering what he had said. Thirty minutes later we found out. He came back in like a tornado and began moving us out. We packed up like Gypsies and hit the road. There were over twenty people in "The Family" now and we all lived out of our cars for the next several days.

One of the couples in "The Family" told a trailer park owner that they were married and needed a place to live. They rented a nice trailer and that night we all moved in. We partied long and hard that summer and were evicted from several places. We finally wised up and split up into smaller groups and found several different houses to rent. Ernie, Jennifer, Jimbo and I found a beautiful three-bedroom house on the beach, and the others found places nearby.

We were always looking for something to get into. During the daytime hours we would run up and down the beach checking out the houses that appeared to be unoccupied. Later at night, we would break in and ransack the houses. Sometimes just for fun and sometimes for profit. One time we broke into a mansion in broad daylight and carried off a television and other smaller appliances. At the time I just looked at it all as innocent fun.

We did all of our grocery shopping together. We would spend about ten dollars for food and walk out with hundreds of dollars worth of stolen goods. We stuffed steaks down our pants and pulled many other sly tricks. We began to slow down a little though when the heat was on. Several friends were busted on the beach and we couldn't afford to let that happen to us again. We limited our drug dealing to the bar and with close friends.

7

Some days my pockets were bulging with money and other days I didn't have a cent. Some days I ate steak and lobster, and other days I had to skip meals. But "The Family" stuck close together and we always tried to provide for each other. We were always partying and making new friends. I remember one girl in particular who stayed with us for a few weeks that summer. She was different from any other girl I had ever met. She claimed to be a witch, but we all laughed at the thought of that. However, she was able to read our palms and tell us things about our lives with amazing accuracy.

One night I let her read my palm and I was startled at all the things she told me. I knew she couldn't have been guessing. As she began to come up to date in my life, she said I would soon be going to court to stand trial for a crime I had committed. As she spoke I could feel the hair stand up on my neck. She told me what day I was going to court and what color suit I would be wearing. At that time I didn't even own a suit. Then came the crusher. She said that everyone would be set free except me. She went on to say that the judge was going to throw the book at me and I would go to prison. I jumped up from my chair and yelled, "You are crazy, witch! I've got this case in the bag. I don't care what you say." However, what she had said really frightened me.

The summer was coming to a close and the beach was soon a much quieter place. The huge crowds had disappeared and only the locals occupied the beach taverns now.

The parties continued, but the change in season brought about changes in attitudes too. Everyone had quit streaking because of the nippy weather. Our drug dealing had toned down considerably. Over the course of the summer, several of our friends had gotten busted, including two more members of "The Family." Several of the guys in "The Family" had received their discharges from the "Corps" and instead of hanging around had packed up and moved back to their home towns.

It was always a sad time when a member of "The Family" would move away. We were a tight group and in our own way we really loved each other and watched out for one another. We were always doing those stupid little things that memories are made of: wearing each other's clothes, taking up for a brother in a fight, lending money we knew we never would see again, sitting patiently while one of our group cried his heart out on your shoulder about some tragedy he was experiencing, or helping a brother or sister to struggle through an overdose. But life goes on. I was continuing my search for true happiness.

One afternoon I was sitting alone on the beach just watching the waves roll in. Seemingly from out of nowhere, a young couple was standing over me and introducing themselves. I invited them to sit and chat awhile and they accepted. It wasn't too long before I found myself in the middle of a conversation about Jesus Christ. I tried to be nice and listen as they talked about finding happiness in Jesus. But the more they talked, the more uneasy I became. I thought to myself that they were real Jesus Freaks! The next thing I knew, they were asking me to pray with them something called a "sinner's prayer" and to be "born again."

Now I had spent most of my childhood in church, but I'd never heard the expression "born again." This whole conversation was beginning to spook me. I stood up and declared that I was thirsty and asked if I could buy them a Coke. They refused, but said they would wait until I came back from getting one. I walked away from them quickly and slipped into the first tavern I could find. I spent the rest of the afternoon drinking beer and watching out the window until that couple finally disappeared. I felt a little guilty about doing that, but I didn't lose any sleep over it. I figured that it was a free country and they could believe what they wanted to and so could I.

Our court date was quickly closing in on us and we received a letter from our lawyer instructing us to drop by and see him. He asked me what I was doing for employment and I told him I was drawing unemployment checks. He said that he thought it might look better if I had a job when I appeared in court, so I began looking around for some work. I came across a construction company that was hiring laborers and was able to get job for Ernie, Jimbo and myself. What a crew we turned out to be. Ernie and Jimbo, because of some past experience, were put on a detail laying blocks while I was jack-of-all-trades and master of none.

We started daily at 6:00 a.m. and usually got all the overtime we wanted, including weekends. We were making lots of money now, but we had no time to party. Then we came up with the idea of doing both. We would eat a tab of acid for breakfast and smoke a couple of joints for lunch. This didn't work out so well. Ernie and Jimbo decided the job was too much like work, so they quit. I decided to stick it out at least until after the trial. It was difficult to get myself up that early every morning. But after a hot cup of coffee and the long drive down the beach I was usually awake enough to punch the time clock when I arrived. Working as a laborer can get pretty boring at times. Everyone is your boss and you usually end up doing nothing by saying that you're doing something for someone else. I worked harder at not working than I did at working.

The day of our trial finally rolled around, October 18, 1973. I didn't have any decent clothes to wear to court so I borrowed a suit from a friend. It didn't really dawn on me until I was seated in the court room that the suit I was wearing was the same color as the palm reader said I would be wearing. I started feeling sick at my stomach. Doc, Rubber, Fuzzy and I sat quietly together. Brad entered the court room with his lawyer and took a seat on the other side of the room. Brad and John had been in jail all summer. I really felt bad about that, but not half as bad as I was going to feel if I got sent to prison as the witch had said I would be. John wasn't there yet and we all wondered where he was. Just before the judge came in I remember looking out the window into the sky and whispering under my breath, "Dear God, if You will get me out of this mess, I promise to try to be a better person for You!"

"Oyez, oyez, oyez, the Superior Court of Carteret Country is now in session, Honorable Judge So and So presiding," and away we went. It wasn't long before we found out that John had already pleaded guilty and was serving a prison sentence, but Brad had decided to fight the case all the way. The day drug on and I heard more lies and cross-lies than I care to remember. Doc and I were called to testify for the state and we told our story just as it had happened. After our testimony, a recess was called and then back into the court room for more of the same.

Finally, a verdict was reached. Doc, Rubber, Fuzzy and I were found not guilty and Brad was sentenced to prison. Brad's lawyer made an immediate appeal, but our lawyer informed us that we were free to go. A sigh of relief came from all of us. We were sternly warned by our lawyer to keep our noses clean, because we were being watched. I felt a new sense of freedom and happiness as I walked out of the court room. Yet, I wondered what the future held in store for me and for "The Family."

I knew that if I stayed around Atlantic Beach much longer, I would be in trouble again and probably worse trouble. I made the decision to quit my job, pack up all my belongings and head back to wild, wonderful West Virginia. We all partied together the last night that I was there, yet there was a sense of sadness in all of us. We all loved each other and knew that it would be a long time, if ever, before we would see each other again. And as everyone knows, it's impossible to relive the past. It's just never quite the same.

The next morning I made my final rounds to say good-by to what was left of "The Family." Then I headed for those country roads that would take me home. The drive back was very lonesome. I was eager to see my parents and old friends in West Virginia, but my eyes filled with tears at every thought of the friends, memories and "The Family" I was leaving in North Carolina. My mind was made up that one day I would return and make new memories. As I drove down the road, I sang the song, "We May Never Pass This Way Again," and wondered what home may have in store for me in my search for happiness.

8

My parents were happy to see me and I moved back into the home place. After being away from home for over three years, there were some difficult adjustments to be made. Mom and Dad had never seen me with long hair and a beard before, and I had accumulated some bad habits that they were finding hard to accept.

It was now winter time and there were no jobs available. I signed up for unemployment checks and loafed. I didn't really want to work anyway. The mountains of West Virginia were majestically beautiful, but I found myself becoming homesick for the beach. I got together with a group of old friends and began to party with them. But it just wasn't the same as partying with "The Family." I was used to partying for days at a time and these guys could barely make it through one night. There was also a shortage of available women. This was one disadvantage that I was not accustomed to. It seemed that all my friends had steady girlfriends and there was none left over for me.

I was slowly becoming very bored with my old home town. One night I was out on the town by myself. I ran into the girlfriend of one of my best friends. I had known her for several years and my friend had informed me that he wanted to marry her. She and I had a few drinks together and talked for quite a while. Later we drove around town in my car and smoked a few joints together. Then she informed me that her boyfriend was out of town for a few days and that she had the keys to his apartment. I immediately picked up on her proposition but I decided to pass it off. I didn't want to lose a good friend over a one-night stand. Over a period of the next several days, she continued to call me on the telephone and we would meet and have drinks together and get high. Finally, temptation became too great and I found myself in my friend's apartment with his girlfriend. As time went by, I lost a good friend and gained a good lover. We began to date steadily. Winter was beautiful in West Virginia. We partied every day and every night. But there was still an emptiness in my heart for the kind of excitement I was accumstomed to in North Carolina. I wasn't happy with my life and I was becoming very restless and eager to travel. Then I ran into my old friend Eddy. We had gone to high school together and he had dropped out of school to enlist in the Marine Corps. It was Eddy who had first gotten me interested in the Marine Corps, and I had enlisted about ten months after he had. Now we were both ex-Marines and he was the closest thing to a brother that I had ever had. We thought alike on many subjects and our Marine Corps background brought us even closer together.

Eddy was now a truck driver for a company in South Carolina. He asked me to ride with him on his next run to Florida and I accepted. He was going to Vero Beach to load a trailer with Indian River citrus fruit and deliver it to some schools in Pennsylvania.

We were driving down around Mount Airy, North Carolina, one morning about 2:00 a.m. when another tractor-trailer eased up alongside of us. I noticed that he was edging over left of center towards us as we were traveling in the passing lane. Eddy had to drop off the shoulder of the road in order to avoid a collision with the other truck. I looked over at Eddy as he began to wrestle with the big steering wheel. I noticed something outside of his window. It was the trailer of our truck. We were jackknifing. Time seemed suspended as we slid across the median strip and across the other lane of traffic. We went crashing through quite a length of guard rails and over a steep embankment.

Finally all was quiet and we sat motionless for what seemed an eternity. They tell me that right before you die, your whole life passes before your eyes. When that truck finally stopped, I'd gotten up to about the eighth grade. The truck was a total mess and diesel fuel was spilled over everything. One little spark and we would have been crispy critters. And yet, Eddy and I crawled out of that wreckage without a scratch on either of us.

There was no traffic on the road so we set out some flares and ran down the road to the nearest phone booth. Eddy called his boss and then the State Police. Then Eddy told me I would have to hitch-hike to a truck stop over a hundred miles away and wait for him there. He didn't want his boss or the police to know that I was in the truck because their insurance didn't cover passengers.

It was very dark and lonely as I walked along the highway. My mind wandered back to the time while I was still in high school and had narrowly escaped death in an automobile accident. I was suddenly brought back to reality when a tractor-trailer roared by me and blew his loud horn. I dived off the side of the road to avoid being run over. Another close call.

Finally I got a ride into Winston-Salem, North Carolina. As I stood at a cross walk preparing to cross I heard a siren blow. I looked up to see a city police car in hot pursuit of a speeder. As the fugitive sped past me, an unnoticing elderly lady drove into the intersection and the police car hit her car broad side at full speed. I stood by helplessly and watched the police car turn end over end three times and come to rest on its wheels. The lady's car spun like a top and stopped several hundred feet down the street. There was nothing I could do but keep on walking. It took me several hours to get to the truck stop that Eddy had told me about. As I sat quietly in a booth and drank coffee, I couldn't shake the thought that someone must be watching over me.

Later that afternoon, Eddy drove into the parking lot with a new truck. We ate dinner and talked about our day's encounters, then it was back in the truck and on the road to Florida. It was a journey with a lot of excitement. We ate a lot of speed and drank a lot of coffee.

We barely escaped two more accidents before arriving safely in Florida. Then after we got our trailer loaded, there was more trouble. These were the days of the truck strikes and we ran into some angry truckers. They weren't hauling anything and they didn't want anyone else to haul anything either. They carried shotguns and pistols and talked real mean. I thought they were going to kill us. They made Eddy pull his truck over and we were shut down until further notice. Somehow after a couple of days we managed to sneak out of town and make our way back up north. When I did get home I made up my mind that truck driving was definitely not my cup of tea. It was good to be with my girlfriend again and just relax and do some partying.

My girlfriend's father worked for the Lockheed-Georgia Aircraft Plant in Clarksburg, West Virginia. He informed me that the company would be hiring workers soon and that I might be able to get a job there. Dating his daughter was getting a little expensive, so I decided to fill out an application for work. I was accepted, but I had to attend a training school every night for a month before I could be hired. During this one-month training period I couldn't see my girlfriend because she was a full-time student during the day and I was in class every night. Because of this situation our relationship suffered.

One day I was in town and happened to meet a really cute girl named Dorlene. She was only four feet eleven inches tall, but I'd never seen so little put together so well. We decided we would make time for each other and began seeing each other on a regular basis. My other girlfriend slowly faded out of the picture. Dorlene lived with her mother and step-father. Her real father lived in Florida. We often talked about how nice it would be to go to Florida and visit her dad and relax on the beach. We both loved the ocean.

I decided to make that dream a reality. I was becoming restless again anyway and my training school was just about over. I put my mind to work on a solution to our problem. I remembered a good friend named Larry who had just come into some money. His leg had been badly injured in a motorcycle accident and his insurance company had just settled with him for quite a large sum. Larry had bought a new car, a large stash of drugs and still had a few thousand dollars put away in the bank. I began to tell him about all the good times I'd had at Atlantic Beach. I told him about the parties and all the pretty girls on the beach. It didn't take long to convince him that we ought to take a little vacation.

Larry and I had three good buddies who had moved to Boynton Beach, Florida, to look for jobs. We heard that they were doing well and I talked Larry into going on to Florida to visit them after we had stayed at Atlantic Beach for awhile. Dorlene's father lived at Pompano Beach, Florida, which was only about twenty-five miles from Boynton. So, I could see that everything should work out smoothly.

We decided to leave for Florida on the night that I graduated from training school. I threw some clothes in a supermarket shopping bag and was ready to roll. As soon as my class was over, Larry and I drove over to Dorlene's house and loaded up the car. We left Clarksburg around midnight and arrived at Atlantic Beach, North Carolina, the next morning. It sure was good to walk barefoot on the sand again and smell that salty breeze blowing in from the ocean. We spent the entire day just relaxing on the beach. It didn't take long to find some old friends to put us up for the night.

Dorlene and I got up early the next morning and drove down to Tommy's Pancake House for breakfast. I often stopped there for breakfast when I worked with the construction company. After breakfast, we took a long romantic walk along the deserted beach. The wind breezed lightly across our faces and blew our hair wildly. The sand and cool morning waters felt good on our bare feet. The air was fresh and full of the sounds and smells of the ocean. The sea gulls lightly floated in the pale blue sky around us. Hand in hand we walked out to the end of fishermen's pier and gazed at the vast amount of water that lay before us. An endless blanket of foamy waves and the briney deep. We sat together and drank in this beautiful picture of morning and fed upon each other's words. There was no doubt in our minds that we were falling in love.

Back at the trailer, the others were just getting up when we returned with Larry's car. We got all of our beach gear together and drove back to the beach for a day of fun in the sun. Later in the day I ran into some members of "The Family." We really rejoiced to see each other. The first thing we did was grab Larry, jump in his car and drive to Fort Macon, an old Civil War fort, and commence to get ourselves loaded. The party had begun and it didn't stop till the day we left for Florida.

Words couldn't express how good it felt to be with Ernie, Jennifer and Jimbo again. They had moved off the beach and found a secluded house about sixty miles away on the other side of New Bern, North Carolina. It was too dangerous to deal drugs on the beach and live there too. Ernie invited us to stay with them while we were in town and we gratefully accepted. That evening we all feasted at a Mexican food restaurant in Havelock. After dinner we drove on to Ernie's house, some fifty miles away. I couldn't forget that drive. When we arrived at Ernie's we discovered that Dorlene had left her purse at the restaurant and I had to drive back and get it. When we finally returned to Ernie's the party was in full swing. What a delight to see more of "The Family" and party again as we had done in the "old days."

Larry was overwhelmed. My friends loved him and he loved them. He became well acquainted with some of my old girlfriends. Larry was ready to retire to Atlantic Beach. He thought it was "party heaven." It made me feel good to know that he was enjoying himself. But now Dorlene was becoming anxious to get to Florida. It really took some talking to convince Larry that we had to go. At first he suggested that Dorlene take a bus, but I talked him out of that. I promised him that we would spend some time partying with "The Family" on our return trip and he finally agreed. I asked Ernie if he could get us some speed for the long drive to Florida, but there was none to be found around the beach that day. So we gratefully accepted Ernie's gift of several tablets of L.S.D. to get us through. The next morning we pointed the car toward Florida, ate the L.S.D. and tripped our trip to the Sunshine State. Sometime later, we somehow arrived safely. I still don't remember how we got there.

Dorlene's father lived in Pompano Beach and our buddies lived at Boynton Beach. Larry let me use his car every day to drive down to see Dorlene. We tried to make the most of our time together. She came up to my buddy's home on several occasions. They had rented a real nice home with a swimming pool. The neighborhood bar was just around the corner and they had plenty of drugs. We spent our days just lying around the pool and getting high. This was truly a hippie's idea of Paradise.

One day I decided to call my parents, just to say hello. What a shock I received. Mom told me that I had a job. This of course, meant that I had to go home. What a bummer! I hated to break the news to Larry, but he was very understanding. We both decided that this job was too good for me to pass up. I also dreaded saying good-by to Dorlene, but she decided to stay in Florida with her father. The next morning Dorlene and I said a sad farewell and Larry and I were back on the road. We did stop in North Carolina for a couple of days on the way back. It was good to party with "The Family" again, and I promised that I would return as soon as possible. As Larry and I crossed the state line into West Virginia, my heart was filled with fear at the thought of settling down to a steady job.

9

The word "work" seemed to take the wind right out of my sails. I had been bumming around for almost a year and the hippie lifestyle really appealed to me. Working in an airplane factory for eight hours a day wasn't my idea of fun. The only fun part was cashing my check on Friday evening and partying with my friends all weekend. Most of my friends were unemployed, but I didn't mind spending my money on them. I knew what it was like to be in their shoes.

I was maintaining correspondence with Dorlene as much as possible. I wrote her letters and sent her flowers now and then. I called her frequently and she called me from time to time too. I would send her money when she needed it and kept hoping that she would come home. I was in need of some real companionship. I tried dating some of the local college girls, but they were just casual friendships. I was living with my parents and at the time, I was making more money than my dad. Yet my parents never asked me for any money to help with expenses. In fact, sometimes my mother would help me out a little after I'd blown my whole paycheck on a weekend fling. At that time, life began to seem so meaningless. I couldn't find any lasting happiness or peace of mind in anyone or anything. Life was really confusing to me.

One sunny Sunday afternoon in July 1974, it appeared that things were beginning to change. I was at the community swimming pool with Casey, one of my best friends. Casey and I had grown up together and we were just like brothers.

We were getting bored just lying in the sun, so we decided to get a volley ball game started. We rented the equipment and made an announcement around the pool that everybody was welcome to join in the game. Several guys and girls came over and soon we had a game under way. Immediately, I notice an attractive young girl whom I had never seen before. She was very appealing to me, not to mention she was quite a volley ball player too. As the afternoon went by I was able to start a conversation with her. Nina was a student at West Virginia University majoring in physical education.

The time went by so quickly and Nina had to go home. We exchanged phone numbers and I promised to call her soon. My heart was excited at the thought of talking to her again. I waited a couple of days and then gave her a call. She sounded genuinely glad to hear from me. After a lengthy conversation, I worked up enough courage to ask her for a date. To my surprise and delight, she accepted. After we hung up, I began to wonder what we could do on our first date. I didn't know what she liked or disliked. I decided to just be myself and hope for the best.

During the summer months, Nina lived with her grandmother in a rural area. She had given me directions over the phone on how to find the house. After several wrong turns I finally found the place and discovered that I was only an hour late. I was nervous about meeting Nina's grandmother. I figured she was a traditional grandmother who didn't like long-haired hippie freaks. But she seemed to accept me right away.

Nina and I left the house and our first date was under way. I decided to take her to The Purple Tree, a night club which featured a live band on weekends. I figured we could drink and dance and get better acquainted. We sat quietly at the table for a few minutes and then I ordered a bourbon on the rocks. I asked Nina what she wanted to drink and she replied, "I don't drink."

"Well, strike one," I thought to myself.

The band had just begun playing so I asked her if she would like to dance. "I don't like to dance," was her reply.

"Strike two," I thought to myself.

Shortly thereafter, we decided to escape the noise and go for a nice quiet drive in the park. I found a secluded place to park the car and we got out to take a walk in the moonlight. We sat together on a picnic table and quietly enjoyed a romantic moment. Then I pulled a joint out of my shirt pocket and lit it up. After a couple of long draws I passed the joint to Nina. Immediately she informed me, "I don't smoke that stuff!"

"Strike three," I said aloud. It was obvious to me that I had struck out with Nina. I offered to take her home and that was the first thing she accepted from me all evening. As I drove away from her grandmother's house, I wondered if I would ever see Nina again. I couldn't help laughing aloud at myself for the way I had totally blown our first date. I really liked her, but we were so different in so many ways. I was really surprised when she agreed to go out with me again. Only from now on, she informed me, the dates would be on her terms.

Nina had a summer job as a swimming instructor at the Clarksburg Y.M.C.A. When I finished my day at the factory, I would stop by the "Y" and wait for her to finish. Then I would drive her home. We would have supper with her grandmother and then spend the rest of the evening together. Every evening was enjoyable and different. We would play tennis, basketball, go swimming or just relax together and watch television. We grew very fond of each other quite quickly. I had dated many girls in the past, but there seemed to be something delightfully different about Nina. I soon found myself telling her that I loved her. This was very much out of character for me. I liked a lot of people, but loved very few. Even more surprising was the fact that she was telling me the same thing. Even my parents noticed a difference in me. I wasn't running around like I used to. I stopped using drugs. I only smoked pot with some close buddies and tried to keep it a secret from Nina. I was actually settling down and enjoying it.

The weeks of that summer seemed to gently glide away and our romance deepened. All too soon the time arrived for Nina to go back to college. We both dreaded the day for we realized it meant that we couldn't see each other as often as we wanted. It was a sad, quiet, fifty-mile drive to the university that day. I helped Nina carry everything into her room in the dormitory. We spent a few moments trying to say good-by before I returned home. The thought of only seeing her on weekends made me very sad. As I drove home alone that night, my heart was in my throat and tears streamed down my face. Somehow, deep down inside of me, I sensed that our relationship would never be the same. When I arrived home, I called Nina to tell her that I loved her and missed her. We talked for an hour.

I lived and worked all week long just thinking about the coming weekend. I could hardly wait to see her darling face and have her close to me again. Our telephone bills were tremendous. Sometimes I just couldn't stand to wait all week to see her. I would drive up to the university in the middle of the week and surprise her. We would usually spend our whole weekend together trying to recapture those magic moments we had shared together during the summer.

But, a memory is a heart warming moment to be remembered and never recaptured. Our love began to fade away as a beautiful ocean sunset, never to be seen again as at first. Our weekends became filled with arguments over trivial things. We became jealous of each other. It seemed that the harder we tried at making it work, the worse it got. We tried desperately to hold on to our relationship. We even discussed marriage as a possible solution to the problem. But, I was too selfish to consider it. Marriage, to me, meant responsibility and I was not ready for that with anybody. I told Nina that I thought marriage was a beautiful institution, but I wasn't ready for an institution yet. When I told her that, it was like throwing water on a dying fire.

A couple of weeks later, Nina informed me on the telephone that our relationship was over and that she didn't want to see me anymore. I had felt that it was coming to this and yet still it was a sudden shock. I also learned that Nina was now seeing a young man at the university. This was like salt in the wound. On top of a broken heart, I also had a hole in my pride and I was leaking all over the place. The only girl who had ever really meant anything to me had left me and found another guy and there was nothing I could do about it. The reality of the whole situation was really beginning to bear down on me. I hadn't really realized how much Nina meant to me until it was too late. I wanted her back no matter what I had to do. I called her and begged her to let me see her again. When I did see her I even got on my knees and proposed marriage to her. Nothing that I said or did would change her mind.

The next several months were a literal living hell for me. I couldn't eat or sleep for thinking about Nina. I lost over twenty pounds. I began to make a lot of mistakes on my job from not concentrating on my work. My fellow employees could tell that something was really bothering me. Sometimes I would even go to the restroom and just sit and cry. I just couldn't get Nina off of my mind. It was now Christmas time and I would be off from work until after New Year's Day. I decided that maybe if I got away for awhile, things would be better. I packed up a few things and went back to North Carolina. I thought that perhaps my old friends could help to cheer me up a little.

Everybody seemed glad to see me and they made me feel right at home. For a little while, the tension of my situation seemed to lift. For a couple of nights I spent some time tending the bar where I used to work. I did it just for old times' sake and it was fun. But once again it was like trying to recapture an old memory. You just can't do it. I partied with members of "The Family" and some old friends and tried to be happy. But my mind and conversation was always drifting back to Nina. My friends could see that I really had a problem. Some of my old girl friends tried to help me get my mind off of Nina, but I harshly rejected them. If I couldn't have Nina then I didn't want anybody. My mind was made up that no one was going to take her place. I honestly tried to explain my feelings to my friends, but no one understood. They would all tell me the same things: "You'll get over it soon," "Someone else will come along," "She's not worth it," etc. I just couldn't accept their advice. I had been through this with other girls too, but never so long and never so severe. I tried to be strong on my own, but this problem was becoming bigger than me. I decided to return home. I had two days left before I had to go back to work.

When I arrived home, my mother could see that I was

in no better spirits than when I had left. She tried her best to comfort me. She suggested that I go to church with her and maybe God would help me with my problems. At this point I was ready to accept help from anybody. I thought about it for awhile and then I made up my mind that maybe God was the answer for Nina and me. I called Nina and begged her for an opportunity to see her again and just talk. After much deliberation she agreed to meet me at her grandmother's house and talk for awhile. When I arrived, we ate lunch and then sat down in the living room for our discussion. I suggested to Nina that God was the answer to our problem and that we should give Him a chance. Finally, Nina confessed to me that she didn't want to hurt me, but she had fallen in love with someone else. She asked me to leave as a friend and I did. It was hard for me to accept, but I had to live with the fact. I was still determined not to give up without a fight. From time to time I would call her and try to persuade her to come back, but it only served to frustrate the matter. I was at a point in my life where nothing seemed to matter to me anymore. I didn't even care about myself. I wondered if I would ever be happy again.

10

One Sunday morning I woke up and decided that I would go to church with my mother. I had such a loneliness in my heart and I was a very unhappy young man. I was really hoping that God would help me get my life straightened out. This was when my search for the reality of God really began.

My dad thought it very strange that out of the clear blue sky I had decided to go to church. He had not attended church since my sister had died fourteen years earlier. While I was at church my dad received a telephone call from Casey, one of my best friends. Dad told Casey that I had gone to church with my mother. Then he added that he hoped the roof didn't fall in and hurt anybody. They both got a good laugh over that one.

Meanwhile, I was sitting in church just as miserable as ever. As I looked around the congregation, it seemed that the same people I knew as a little boy were sitting in the same pews with the same sour expressions on their faces. The same men were standing outside between services and smoking their cigarettes. Everything seemed so pious and artificial. I made up my mind right then and there I was not coming back to that church again. When we arrived home, I informed my mother that maybe religion was alright for her, but it certainly wasn't my "bag." I decided to set out on a search to find God on my own. I figured that the logical place to find out about God would be in the Bible. So every night I would lock myself in the bathroom and read the Bible. I started reading in the beginning with the book of Genesis. I couldn't make heads or tails out of what I was reading. Soon it became boring and I stopped reading somewhere in the book of Leviticus. I tried praying and talking with God, but I figured for some reason He just didn't hear me. He never answered me the way He did Moses.

Then I got a real brainstorm. I remembered that when my sister died, my Sunday School teacher told me that Pam went to heaven to be with God. I figured that I had at least one person up there who was on my side. Maybe

Pam could get God's attention for me.

Late one evening I drove to the graveyard and found my sister's grave. In desperation I literally threw myself upon her grave and began to cry and plead with God to help me. I even thought that perhaps my sister could hear me. I began to plead with her, "Pam, I know you are in heaven and God loves you, but I'm down here and I've really made a mess of my life. I'm so sorry. Could you please talk to God for me and see if He will do something to help me. Please tell Him I'm sorry about all those broken promises I made to Him, but I just couldn't help myself. Please, please help me Pammy." Then I told her all about Nina and how I felt in my heart.

God only knows how long I lay on that grave and what all I said. Finally, I pulled myself together and got back to my car. I drove away just as miserable as when I'd come, having accomplished nothing. I wondered to myself if maybe I was going crazy. Certainly, I figured no sane man would put himself through all of this over some woman. There had to be an easier way to reach God.

Over a period of the next several weeks I began to listen to a preacher on my car radio. He came on the air at midnight and talked about the Bible for half an hour. Some times I would be so drunk or high on drugs that I would pass out before the preacher finished his message, but I listened faithfully every night. He talked about Jesus Christ as though the two of them were good buddies. He mentioned that God wanted our lives to be filled with peace and happiness and joy. He made it all sound so simple that I guess I just tripped all over it, but couldn't seem to find it. I laid my hand on my car radio like he said and prayed with him, but at that time it didn't seem to do anything for me. I just became more discouraged. I began to wonder if there really was a God or was it all just another money-making racket.

Then I wondered if maybe I could find God in nature. God had supposedly created everything. Maybe I could find Him in His creation. I remembered that when I was in high school I used to spend a lot of time alone in the woods. I always felt close to God there. At least it was worth a try. One Saturday morning, I decided to take a long walk in the woods behind my parents' house. I took my shotgun along with me in hopes that I might bag a few squirrels. What a beautiful day it was. The woods were filled with the sounds and smells of nature. I found a pleasant spot and took a seat upon a log. As I gazed off into the woodland beauty my thoughts began to drift back to the carefree days of my boyhood. How innocent I had once been. I had been a gullible young lad and easily led astray. I had been very inquisitive about life and things. I remembered word for word the poem I had written entitled "The Question" and my many escapades trying to find an answer to that question.

Then my thinking began to become a little more critical. I surveyed my life and found it was not a very pretty picture. Recently, I had lost two very close friends in automobile accidents. The experience had made death so much more real to me. These friends were my age. Why did they have to die? Why did Nina have to leave me? Why did I ever start using drugs? Why wouldn't God talk to me? Why didn't anybody understand me? Why had I given my parents such a hard time all my life? Why was I such a brat? Why? Why? Why? Really now, what was life all about? Were we all born into this world just to go to school, get a job, find a wife, have kids, get old and die? There must be more to this rat race called life than this.

I quietly sat pondering these questions over and over again. The stillness of the forest offered no solutions. I looked down at the shotgun that lay across my lap. Now there is a solution, I thought. Why not? I could certainly end it all in less than a second and probably wouldn't experience any pain. I began to wrestle with the thought over and over again in my mind. Why not? Suddenly, almost without control of myself, I had the muzzle of the gun in my mouth. I had cocked the hammer back with my finger and my thumb was on the trigger. It would all be over now in just a flash. My mind began to race over the years of my life and a voice from somewhere seemed to taunt me, "Pull the trigger, pull the trigger." I tried to pull that trigger. Suddenly I froze from within. One thing stood between me and death. I was frozen from the fear of the hereafter. I believed in heaven and I believed in hell. Where would I go? The compulsion to die was strong and I tried again, but with the same results. I was a failure. I couldn't even die successfully. Oh, how miserable life had become.

After that experience my parents watched me go from bad to worse. Rebellion, bitterness, and hatred seemed to possess me. I began to drink heavily and waste my money on drugs again. I gave up about caring for anything or anybody, including myself.

My friend, Larry, and I became constant companions again. We were always high on something. Many times we would get together on a Friday evening and take some T.H.C. or "drop some reds" and lose our minds for awhile. Sometimes we would wake up the next day in some part of town with no idea how we got there, where we had been or what we had done. Once a young lady approached me on the street and without warning began to slap my face. She said that the night before I had beaten her up. To my knowledge, I'd never seen her before in my life. After some quick explaining and an apology, we became close friends and later one of my best friends married her.

Life was still an endless search for meaning and no answers. My friends told me that at the rate I was going, I would soon be addicted to drugs. How foolish, I thought. I can quit this stuff any time I want to. I just don't want to. I thought of Nina often, and wondered if I could ever really be happy again.

11

There was a revival being held at the church which my mother attended. Mom would daily encourage me to go to the meetings with her. She said that the evangelist was an exciting young lady named Rita who played the piano, sang and preached wonderful sermons every evening. After much persuasion from my mother, I decided to attend one of the meetings. I came to that decision for two reasons: one, to get my mother off my back; and two, because I had never seen a woman preacher before. Mom had told me so much about Rita that I wanted to see for myself if it were so. Lately, I had been so depressed with living that anything would be a welcome change.

There definitely was something different about Rita. She seemed to radiate as she sang, played the piano and preached. She was exciting and I thought the excitement was contagious. As she played the piano and sang, I wanted to clap my hands and stamp my feet. As I looked around at the rest of the congregation, I became thoroughly disgusted. They just sat there and looked at Rita like an old cow staring at a new gate. I figured this young lady needed a little help. Before I knew what I was doing, I was up on my feet! To the utter amazement of the congregation and total embarrassment of my mother, I said, "Why don't we all get up off of our bases and sing along?" Then I began to clap my hands and sing the chorus that Rita was leading. To my surprise, one by one, the whole congregation stood to their feet, clapped their hands and began to sing along.

Later, Rita preached a good sermon about how we can be born again by faith in Jesus Christ. Then she gave a good old-fashioned altar call and asked people to come forward and accept Jesus Christ as their personal Savior. I really wanted to go forward that night and accept Christ, but pride and stubbornness prevented me. When the meeting was dismissed, I hung around and waited for an opportunity to talk with Rita. I asked her where she attended church regularly. She told me that she attended a little Full Gospel non-denominational church in

Clarksburg which was about fifteen miles east of where my parents lived. She also gave me directions on how to get there and I assured her that I would be there on the following Sunday.

As I was leaving the church building that night, I was approached by one of the elderly ladies of the congregation. She poked her finger in my chest, looked me squarely in the eye and said, "Young man, just because you look like Jesus doesn't mean you are!" I suppose she was referring to my long hair and beard and my boldness. She didn't have to worry about my disrupting any more services in that church. I had no intention of returning. I wanted to attend some place where there was a little life.

The following Sunday I was able to find the little church in Clarksburg where Rita attended. From the time I walked in the door, until the time I walked out, I was made to feel welcome there. People were shaking my hand, patting me on the back, and saying, "Praise the Lord, Brother!" I didn't know one person there and Rita wasn't there either, yet I felt right at home. No one seemed to notice my long hair or my beard or the way I dressed. They just welcomed me and accepted me the way I was. I remember saying to myself, "This is the place for me!" People sang and clapped and raised their hands and some were even laughing for joy. I had never experienced anything like this before, especially in a church. Yet deep down inside of me, I knew this was a place where I could find God. On my way home from the services, I made up my mind that this was going to be the church I attended from now on. I remember that I was so excited I smoked a joint on the way home to celebrate my new discovery.

I had only been attending this Full Gospel church for a couple of weeks when they had a special guest speaker one Sunday morning. His name was John Gimenez and he was the pastor of a church in Virginia Beach called the Rock Church. He was a lot like Rita in that he was very enthusiastic and exciting. But his message was a little different from Rita's. This man stood in front of the congregation and told how he had been a drug addict, an alcoholic and a criminal before he had surrendered his life to Jesus Christ. Now this caught my attention from the very start. I figured that this guy and I had something in common. He talked about how miserable his life had been. Oh how I could relate to that! Then he went on to tell how he had come to the place in his life where he had decided that if Jesus Christ was real, he was willing to give Him a chance. He said that he had accepted Jesus Christ as his personal Savior and that Jesus had literally transformed his life and made him into a new person. Then he explained this transformation by reading a verse of scripture from the Bible found in 2 Corinthians 5:17: *Therefore if any man is in Christ, he is a new creature; the old things passed away; behold, new things have come.*

John went on to explain that this experience with Jesus was available to anyone who wanted a new start in life. My heart began to throb within me and I hung onto his every word. As he ended his sermon he asked everyone to bow their heads and to close their eyes for just a moment. As I sat there in silence I began to reflect on my past life. I needed a fresh start in life and God knew I wanted a new beginning. But no one had ever effectively explained to me how I could have this new beginning. My thoughts were interrupted by the sound of John's voice: "If anyone here would like to know Jesus and have a new start in life, please raise your hand and I will pray for you."

I opened one eye and peeped around to make sure that nobody was watching me. Then I reluctantly raised my hand and quickly lowered it again. I didn't want anyone to know that I had a problem. Then to my surprise John asked for everyone who had raised their hands to please get up from their seats and come forward to the altar and he would pray with them. I felt as though I had been tricked and I didn't like it one little bit. My pride and stubbornness once again held me in my seat as others went forward for prayer. Then the real shocker came. John pointed at me and said, "Son, I believe your hand was raised, will you come?"

Embarrassment, fear and anger all began to boil

within me. "Who does he think he is?" I thought to myself. I had been involved in many forms of mischief in my life, but one thing I had never done was poke a preacher in the nose. I figured there was a first time for everything and now was the time. I felt insulted and angered and I was going to get even. I got out of my seat and went forward with every intention of poking that preacher in the nose. But when I got to that altar, something happened.

As I stood there John walked in front of me and seemed to instinctively grab my hands in his. Then he looked me squarely in the eyes and told me that God really loved me and was personally concerned about me. I needed to hear that and I desperately wanted to believe it. He went on to tell me that God loved me so very much that He sent His only Son into the world to die for my sins. He said that Jesus was my substitute. I should have died on a cross but Jesus took my place because He loved me. He said that God's love for me was so great that if I were the only person on the earth, Jesus would have come and done it all just for me.

Now at that time, I really didn't understand everything John was telling me. But his sincerity and warmth and the love that I felt as he spoke to me was enough to tell my heart that what he was saying was the truth, whether I completely understood it or not. Then he looked at me earnestly and said, "Son, you must be born again!"

"How do I do that?" I questioned.

John opened his Bible to the tenth chapter of the book of Romans and read to me verses eight through eleven:

"The word is near you, in your mouth and in your heart" — *that is, the word of faith which we are preaching,*

that if you confess with your mouth Jesus as Lord, and believe in your heart that God raised Him from the dead, you shall be saved;

for with the heart man believes, resulting in righteousness, and with the mouth he confesses, resulting in salvation.

For the Scripture says, "Whoever believes in Him will not be disappointed."

That all sounded pretty good to me, but how did I know if it were talking about me, I questioned. Then John read to me verse thirteen: *For "Whoever will call upon the name of the Lord will be saved."* Then John assured me that "whoever" included me! The only thing left to do was for me to believe it and act upon it by confessing it with my mouth. I decided then and there that I too would give Jesus Christ a chance to help me. I knelt down at the altar and bowed my head with John. Then I repeated after him what he called a "sinner's prayer." It sounded something like this:

"Heavenly Father, I come to You humbly now in the name of the Lord Jesus Christ. I confess to You that I am a sinner. I am truly sorry for my sins. With Your help, I now repent from all my sins. I believe and confess that Jesus Christ is Lord and that You raised Him from the dead. I believe that the blood of Jesus Christ, God's Son, cleanses me now from all sin.

"Lord Jesus, come into my heart now and be my personal Savior and change my life for good and I will serve You forever! Thank You, Lord Jesus, amen."

When I opened my eyes and looked up I saw John smiling at me. He said, "Praise the Lord, Brother, now by faith, you are saved!" Well, that was all fine and dandy, I figured. But I didn't feel any different than I did before I prayed.

"What do you mean, I'm saved by faith? What is faith anyway?"

Once again John opened his Bible. This time he read to me from Hebrews 11:1: *Now faith is the assurance of things hoped for, the conviction of things not seen.*

"That sounds good too, man, but can you explain it to me?" I asked.

John went on to explain that having faith meant to be firmly persuaded that what we want to happen will actually take place and what we are earnestly hoping for is actually waiting for us up ahead. This helped me to understand a little better. But now I wondered if I had any of this faith or not.

Every time I had a question, John would answer that

question by opening his Bible and reading to me. This time he read to me from Romans 12:3: *God has allotted to each a measure of faith.* It made me feel good to know that I had something that I didn't know I had. John explained to me that faith is a little like discovering a muscle that you didn't know you had. Once you find it, you can exercise it and it becomes stronger and more dependable with use. You exercise your faith by reading God's Word and acting upon what it says; in other words, by being a doer of God's Word. Then he showed me Romans 10:17: *So faith comes from hearing, and hearing by the word concerning Christ.*

John said that if I wanted to grow in faith, I would have to start studying the Bible every day. I agreed that I would read my Bible. I shook John's hand and started back to my seat. I really didn't feel any different, but he said that I wasn't saved by my feelings. I was saved by hearing what the Word of God said and choosing to believe it and act upon it. As I walked the aisle back to my seat you would have thought that the congregation had gotten saved instead of me. They were smiling and clapping their hands and saying, "Congratulations, praise the Lord, Brother!" I did begin to feel strangely warm and more than ever, accepted. This was only the beginning of a whole new way of life for me and I was to find out that everything doesn't happen just overnight.

As I began to read my Bible every day I became aware that there were a lot of things in my life that were going to have to change. I began to wonder if I could really stick it out or not. It was definitely a challenge. I really wanted to go to heaven someday, and it scared me to think of hell.

At this point in my Christian experience I was serving the Lord more out of a fear of going to hell than out of a love for Him and His mercy. To me, salvation was more of a "fire insurance" than a blessed assurance. I wanted to be happy and free like the other Christians in that church appeared to be, but I just didn't feel that way on the inside.

Then one morning as I was reading my Bible before going to work, I came across John 8:31,32,36:
Jesus therefore was saying to those Jews who had believed

Him, *"If you abide in My word, then you are truly disciples of Mine;*

and you shall know the truth, and the truth shall make you free . . . .

"If therefore the Son shall make you free, you shall be free indeed."

I knew in my heart that this was God's way of telling me that if I truly wanted to be free and to feel free, I wouldn't give up. I must continue with Him regardless of my feelings or the circumstances that would confront me. I decided that morning to continue with Jesus and give Him the opportunity to make me free indeed.

12

I had begun to attend services regularly and to read my Bible daily. I found the Bible to be difficult to understand at first. At the advice of some older Christians, I bought a paraphrased edition of the Bible and read it along with the King James version. This seemed to help me greatly in understanding some of the more difficult passages.

I found myself talking more and more openly to people about Jesus Christ and His saving grace. This caused several of my friends to feel uneasy around me. Other friends would defend me by saying that my experience was just a stage in life I was going through and soon I would be back to normal again. I told my friends that they needed to be "born again" also, but none were interested enough to give it a try.

Although at first I wasn't much of a shining example to them, I did talk a lot about Jesus. I believed in my heart that I was a Christian, but I hadn't yet completely given up my old style of living. I still had the same old friends. I still frequently visited the local bars and had a couple of drinks from time to time. I still liked to smoke a joint occasionally with my buddies. However, these things began to make me uneasy on the inside and my very presence and conversation seemed to make my old friends feel ill at ease around me. I was straddling a fence and fighting a battle in my mind over which way I should jump. I knew I must make a decision soon or I would go crazy. I loved my friends and didn't want to lose them, and yet deep inside of me I knew that the Lord must be number one in my life if I were ever going to be truly happy and stay that way.

One day while reading my Bible, I came across Matthew 3:13-17:

Then Jesus arrived from Galilee at the Jordan coming to John, to be baptized by him.

But John tried to prevent Him, saying, "I have need to be baptized by You, and do You come to me?"

But Jesus said to him, "Permit it at this time; for in this way it is fitting for us to fulfill all righteousness." Then he permitted Him.

And after being baptized, Jesus went up immediately from the water; and behold, the heavens were opened, and He saw the Spirit of God descending as a dove, and coming upon Him,

and behold, a voice out of the heavens, saying, "This is My beloved Son, in whom I am well-pleased."

I remembered as a little boy I had attended Vacation Bible School at the Baptist church. I had always thought that they called John, the Baptist, because he was a member of the Baptist church. I also remembered that as a little boy I had been water baptized along with some other youths in a river near our home. I never really understood why I was baptized or what it meant. I just did it because my friends were doing it. Now I began to question why we should be baptized. I noticed from the scriptures that our Heavenly Father was well pleased when Jesus was baptized. I wanted Him to be well pleased with me too.

The following Sunday I went to church with the intention of asking my pastor what water baptism was all about. Before I ever got a chance to talk to him, he announced from the pulpit that the next Sunday afternoon there would be a water baptismal service for all who needed to be baptized. It almost seemed to me that the Lord was setting me up for something.

The week rolled by quickly and the next Sunday afternoon found me standing on the river bank at Center Branch listening to Pastor Wilson read from the book of Romans, chapter six, verses three through eleven:

Or do you not know that all of us who have been baptized into Christ Jesus have been baptized into His death?

Therefore we have been buried with Him through baptism into death, in order that as Christ was raised from the dead through the glory of the Father, so we too might walk in newness of life.

For if we have become united with Him in the likeness of His death, certainly we shall be also in the likeness of His resurrection,

knowing this, that our old self was crucified with Him, that our body of sin might be done away with, that we should no longer be slaves to sin;

for he who has died is freed from sin.

Now if we have died with Christ, we believe that we shall also live with Him,

knowing that Christ, having been raised from the dead, is never to die again; death no longer is master over Him.

For the death that He died, He died to sin, once for all; but the life that He lives, He lives to God.

Even so consider yourselves to be dead to sin, but alive to God in Christ Jesus.

As I listened to the pastor explain these verses, I could see that I really needed to obey the scriptures. God is pleased with obedience. Pastor Wilson went on to say that many people didn't take water baptism very seriously, but that Jesus said in Mark 16:15-16: *"Go into all the world and preach the gospel to all creation. He who has believed and has been baptized shall be saved; but he who has disbelieved shall be condemned."*

After we had received some more instructions about water baptism, those of us who needed to be baptized were taken one by one into the river and immersed.

When I came up out of the waters, I just knew in my heart that with God's help I was going to walk in newness of life. As I walked along the river bank I was greeted by one of the elders of the church. His name was Ken and he wanted to congratulate me on my baptism. The he said that he wanted to read to me a verse of scripture found in Acts, chapter two, verse thirty-eight: *"Repent, and let each of you be baptized in the name of Jesus Christ for the forgiveness of your sins; and you shall receive the gift of the Holy Spirit."*

After reading the scripture to me, he asked me if I would like to receive the gift of the Holy Spirit. I had never been a person who would turn down a gift, but what in the world was the Holy Spirit? Ken replied, "The Holy Spirit is not a *what*, but rather a *who*. The gift of the Holy Spirit is often referred to as the baptism in the Holy Spirit." He then read to me from Matthew 3:11: *"As for me, I baptize you with water for repentance, but He who is coming after me is mightier than I, and I am not fit to remove His sandals; He will baptize you in the Holy Spirit and fire."*

Ken then explained to me that the Holy Spirit was the

third person of the trinity of God. The Holy Spirit would strengthen me, comfort me and give me supernatural ability to accomplish tasks that God would give me to do. One of the reasons Jesus Christ came was to immerse people into the power of the Holy Spirit. Then Ken read to me Acts 1:8: *"But you shall receive power when the Holy Spirit has come upon you; and you shall be My witnesses both in Jerusalem, and in all Judea and Samaria, and even to the remotest part of the earth."*

At this point Pastor Wilson entered into the conversation. He said that the gift of the Holy Spirit was first of all given on what the Church calls the day of Pentecost, over nineteen hundred years ago. Then he opened his Bible and read to us Acts 2:1-4:

And when the day of Pentecost had come, they were all together in one place.

And suddenly there came from heaven a noise like a violent rushing wind, and it filled the whole house where they were sitting.

And there appeared to them tongues as of fire distributing themselves, and they rested on each one of them.

And they were all filled with the Holy Spirit and began to speak with other tongues, as the Spirit was giving them utterance.

All of these things sounded exciting. I knew that if I was going to continue to be a Christian I needed some kind of power other than myself. At times, I would even feel bitter toward God because I felt He was expecting too much from me. I decided then and there that I wanted to experience this baptism in the Holy Spirit. I needed His power to help me make it through the tough times. Then I asked Pastor Wilson if people today could actually have this experience with the Holy Spirit. Without a hesitation he read to me Acts 2:39: *"For the promise is for you and your children, and for all who are far off, as many as the Lord our God shall call to Himself."*

He assured me that I was one of the "all" who were far off. My next question was, "How do I receive this baptism in the Holy Spirit?" Ken then read to me Luke 11:9-13:

"And I say to you, ask, and it shall be given to you; seek, and you shall find; knock, and it shall be opened to you.

"For eveyone who asks, receives; and he who seeks, finds; and to him who knocks, it shall be opened.

"Now suppose one of your fathers is asked by his son for a fish; he will not give him a snake instead of a fish, will he?

"Or if he is asked for an egg, he will not give him a scorpion, will he?

"If you then, being evil, know how to give good gifts to your children, how much more shall your heavenly Father give the Holy Spirit to those who ask Him?"

Pastor Wilson then read to me Acts 19:6: *And when Paul laid his hands upon them, the Holy Spirit came on them, and they began speaking with tongues and prophesying.*

The only thing left for me to do was ask the Lord Jesus to baptize me in the Holy Spirit. Pastor Wilson and Ken said they would lay their hands on me and pray for me to receive. As they laid their hands on me and prayed I could sense a stirring from deep within. Then I began to move my lips and make a noise. As I did this, the Holy Spirit began to give me an utterance and I was speaking in other tongues. It was a heavenly language. I'd never heard anything like it. I began to sense the presence of God like I had never felt before. I knew He was in me and with me now. It was a very real and yet personal experience.

Some days later, I noticed that I had a new love growing inside of me. I saw things differently. I looked at people differently. I was better able to control my temper and my tongue now. I had a new love for the Bible and it seemed that the Bible was becoming easier for me to understand and put together now. This baptism in the Holy Spirit was slowly but surely bringing about some marvelous changes in me.

13

I had become a member of the Clarksburg Y.M.C.A. while Nina was a swimming instructor there. I thought that perhaps I would see her from time to time and maybe re-establish our friendship. After taking karate classes for several months I discovered that I had developed an abdominal hernia. I visited a local surgeon and he scheduled me for an operation. He suggested that perhaps I should take a couple of weeks' vacation before the operation because I would be laid up for several weeks after surgery. This was discouraging to me because I had had this operation once before. While I was in the Marine Corps I had developed a hernia while lifting weights and was placed in the Naval Hospital at Cherry Point, North Carolina for surgery. It was almost three months before I could return to full duty. I knew this operation wasn't going to be any fun so I decided to accept the doctor's suggestion and take two weeks' vacation. My first thought was to go back to Atlantic Beach, North Carolina, and tell all my old friends about the Lord Jesus Christ.

My operation was scheduled for the first week of August 1975, so I took the last two weeks of July for my vacation. A good friend of mine, Dave, decided to make the trip with me. Although Dave was not a born-again Christian, he was willing to listen and discuss the Bible as we drove along. We arrived at Atlantic Beach just after noon on a beautiful sunshiny day. The first thing we did was look up my old friend, Toby, to see if he could find us a place to stay for a few days.

Toby was more than happy to let us stay in the trailer he was renting. He would be working out of town for a couple of weeks and said that Dave and I could have the trailer to ourselves. After unpacking and freshening up a bit, Dave and I headed for the bar where I used to work. I figured that most of my old friends and some of "The Family" would still be hanging around there. My guess was correct and we had a very happy reunion. I felt a different kind of love for these old friends. It was more of a compassion than anything else. I knew I was looking at them through the eyes of Jesus Christ and seeing human beings who needed God's love and God's help to solve their deep-seated problems.

In my heart I felt an urgency to tell them about my new experience with Jesus Christ. Oh how they all needed to know and experience the love of Jesus in their lives. They had welcomed me with open arms and it felt so good to be accepted by them. Now was the time, I thought, to share my newly found faith with them. They all listened intently as I told them what had happened to me. They all agreed that they were happy for me. They all agreed that they needed a change in their lives. But they all voiced their feelings as follows: "We love you, Brother, and we're happy to see you again, but please leave your pulpit at home!"

I felt crushed. How could they say such a thing? Didn't they know that I loved them and wanted only the best for them? For the rest of the afternoon, I felt confused and bewildered. That night, all my old friends got together for a party. I knew what would happen if I went to that party. But out of a sense of obligation, I went. Everybody was getting high on something. I pretended to enjoy myself but on the inside I was miserable. My mind kept drifting off to Jesus, Jesus, Jesus. I tried to act happy and have fun with my old friends but I knew I was a different person. I just couldn't live the old life anymore.

The next day we went to the beach and lay in the sun. I watched the ocean waves roll in and my thoughts were turned to Jesus. I couldn't shake it. I walked along the street and noticed my own image in a picture window. I looked like the same person on the outside but on the inside I knew I was different. Later that day several friends followed me into the local barber shop and watched as I got shaved for the first time in two years. I spent the next several days wandering around the beach trying to set things straight in my mind. I knew that I had had an experience with the Lord but it seemed I had left all that back in West Virginia. And yet, it was haunting me here and now. "What do I do?" I thought.

The night before Dave and I were to return home,

there was a big party planned. As usual, there were plenty of drugs and drinks and rock music. But this night and this party were destined to be different for me. In my weakness I endulged in all the activities. But nothing seemed to affect me as it once did. I wasn't getting high. At one point in the evening I stood silently by myself. I quietly observed my friends as they endulged in their merrymaking. Some were lying on the floor and some were sitting in the traditional cross-legged position. They all had bloodshot eyes. The room was enveloped with a thick cloud of marijuna smoke. As my eyes wondered from face to face I could hear a voice softly speaking to me from deep within, "Look around and observe. Is this what you want for your life?" I questioned myself at this point. I had given several years of my life to this kind of living and had not found true happiness or peace of mind. It had been a continual struggle to be accepted by everybody and a growing fear of being busted again, a fear of being caged like some animal in a jail somewhere to be forgotten forever. Man surely wasn't made to spend his life in an endless struggle for happiness and acceptance, was he?

A period of silence went by as I pondered my own questions. Then the soft voice from within seemed to challenge me, *"Call to Me, and I will answer you, and I will tell you great and mighty things, which you do not know."* It wasn't until much later that I found those words contained in scripture in the book of Jeremiah, chapter thirty-three, verse three. I made the decision that night that I wanted to see and experience those great and mighty things the Lord was talking about. The next morning Dave and I left North Carolina and I said good-by to my old friends and my old life.

The next Sunday morning found me listening intently to the sermon. Deep inside of me I felt guilty because I knew I had sinned while I was in North Carolina. At the end of his sermon Pastor Wilson read from 1 John 1:6-9:

If we say that we have fellowship with Him and yet walk in the darkness, we lie and do not practice the truth;

but if we walk in light as He Himself is in the light, we have fellowship with one another, and the blood of Jesus, His Son cleanses us from all sin.

If we say that we have no sin, we are deceiving ourselves, and the truth is not in us.

If we confess our sins, He is faithful and righteous to forgive us our sins and to cleanse us from all unrighteousness.

Then he said that if any of us had sinned we needed to confess our sins to the Lord and receive His forgiveness. At that point I knew that I needed forgiveness for what I had done in North Carolina. I turned to a man in the congregation named Charlie Reich and asked him to pray with me. I told him what I had done and we prayed together and asked the Lord to forgive me. When we had finished praying, I felt the guilty feelings leave me and I knew I was forgiven. It was a wonderful, peaceful feeling.

The next day I was lying on my hospital bed and staring at the ceiling. I had been prepared for surgery and my mind was drifting back to the first time I had had this same operation. This time I wasn't fearful. My thoughts were interrupted as Pastor Wilson entered the room and proclaimed "Praise the Lord!" He came to pray with me before I went to surgery. He assured me that I had nothing to worry about, and the Lord had everything under control. Then he opened his Bible and read to me from James 5:14-15:

Is anyone among you sick? Let him call for the elders of the church, and let them pray over him, anointing him with oil in the name of the Lord;

and the prayer offered in faith will restore the one who is sick, and the Lord will raise him up, and if he has committed sins, they will be forgiven him.

He then anointed me with oil in the name of the Lord Jesus Christ and prayed a prayer of faith. Shortly thereafter I was taken to surgery. I remember waking up in my room again as the anesthesia was wearing off. I was feeling no pain. I could hear Pastor Wilson explaining to me, "Sometimes God intervenes with a miracle of healing, and sometimes He allows the doctors to do the work. But in either case, the Lord is in control and we praise Him for the results." I was walking around the hospital that same evening and the doctor released me to go home in two days. I was back to work within two weeks and my doctor said I had healed incredibly fast.

At this time I was still living with my parents and driving a good distance to work every day and church on weekends. I also decided to take advantage of my G.I. benefits and enrolled in some night classes at the Clarksburg campus of Salem College. I had thought that I wanted to earn a degree in real estate and perhaps have my own real estate brokerage. All of this caused a lot of rushing and running around. I decided it was time to move out of my parents' home and find an apartment in Clarksburg. I found a nice duplex apartment in a convenient location. One of my closest friends named Casey decided to move in with me and divide the cost of living. We had grown up together and were as close as brothers. We got along great except for the fact that Casey wasn't a Christian, and he showed no interest in becoming one. We also got along fine with our neighbors except that they found us a little hard to figure out. On Friday nights, Casey would have his friends over for a party. The neighbors would watch as the people came in with their bottles and the rock music would blare throughout the neighborhood. On Saturday nights my friends would come over for a prayer meeting. The neighbors would watch as the people came in with their Bibles and guitars and the air was filled with gospel music. I knew the neighbors must have wondered what kind of beliefs we had. Since I had returned from North Carolina, the Lord had delivered me from the desire to smoke marijuana and drink wine. I knew as the weeks rolled by that my relationship with Jesus was becoming more stable. His love and mercy were sustaining me.

14

January 1976 rolled around pretty quickly and I decided my New Year's Resolution would be to have a closer relationship with my Lord Jesus. The Lord had been so good to me and I wanted to learn all I could about Him in order to help other people. I would often become frustrated over my lack of knowledge of the Bible, but I continued to pray and to ask the Lord to help me communicate my faith in Him to other people.

I had some vacation time coming, so I decided I would us the second week of January to visit a friend who was in full-time ministry in Columbus, Ohio. I had met Victor Maldonaldo while he was preaching in Clarksburg, West Virginia. Victor was the director of a ministry in Columbus called Outreach For Youth. This ministry was geared toward helping young people with any kind of problem, and teaching them that the Lord Jesus Christ can help them in all of their problems. I wanted to spend some time there with Victor and learn how to help and counsel with young people. It was an exciting experience to see how Jesus was changing young lives just as He had changed, and was changing, mine.

While I was in Columbus I told Victor that I was sharing an apartment in Clarksburg with a life-long friend who wasn't a Christian. Casey was a good person, but he wasn't yet born again. Ever since my conversion I had been praying that Casey would surrender his life to Jesus also, but he just wasn't very interested at that time.

Victor seemed to be quite concerned about the whole situation.

"Dan, you are not living in a very good circumstance at this time," he told me.

"What do you mean?" I questioned.

Immediately Victor got his Bible out and read to me 2 Corinthians 6:14-18:

Do not be bound together with unbelievers; for what partnership have righteousness and lawlessness, or what fellowship has light with darkness?

Or what harmony has Christ with Belial, or what has a

believer in common with an unbeliever?

Or what agreement has the temple of God with idols? For we are the temple of the living God; just as God said, "I will dwell in them and walk among them; and I will be their God, and they shall be My people.

"Therefore, come out from their midst and be separate," says the Lord. "And do not touch what is unclean; and I will welcome you.

"And I will be a father to you, and you shall be sons and daughters to Me," says the Lord Almighty.

Victor said, "If you are sharing an apartment with an unbeliever, then you are living in a divided house and a divided house cannot stand very long."

"Please explain a little more, Victor," I urged.

"Well, Dan," he said, "I know you love the Lord and want to live for Him."

"That's right," I agreed.

"But, you are a young Christian and not too strong yet in the ways of the Lord. You are living in a situation where you are constantly being tempted to slip back into your old life-style. If you should happen to backslide at this point in your Christian life, you might never be able to forgive yourself and come back to Jesus. You need to separate yourself from your unbelieving friends for awhile until you are strong enough in the Lord to be able to help them."

This advice seemed rather stern to me at first, but later I learned how true it really is. I enjoyed my visit to Ohio and returned home with Victor's advice laying heavily upon my heart.

Casey and I had always been the very best of friends, but since I had become a Christian we didn't seem to have much in common any longer. In fact, we were finding it difficult to even carry on any kind of conversation. I always wanted to talk about Jesus and he didn't want to listen. I really cared about his soul, but I wasn't mature enough yet to know how to effectively communicate God's love to him. I could see that Victor was right. Our house was slowly dividing.

One night I was home alone and reading my Bible. I

got tired early and decided to go to bed. I had been asleep only a short time when I was awakened by the sound of our front door opening and closing. I supposed that it was Casey coming home because the front door was locked and he was the only person other than myself who had a key. As I lay quietly, I could hear footsteps coming across the living room floor toward my room. I was lying on my side with my back toward the bedroom door. As I listened, I could hear my door slowly being opened. Suddenly, for no apparent reason, I began to feel fear rising up from deep within me. I could hear someone breathing heavily as he stood in my doorway. I felt such a fear rising within me that I was not able to turn over to look at whoever was there. I felt frozen in place and a heavy cloud of coldness seemed to fill my room. I was aware that the breathing noise was growing louder and getting closer to me. I felt a pressure building up inside of me and coming to a head. I opened my mouth to scream, but nothing came out. I was literally paralyzed with fear. The breathing noise came so close that I could actually feel the warm breath upon my neck.

Finally the scream that I was searching for came out and I shot up out of my bed as though it were a trampoline. I whirled around to see who was there and found no one. I flipped on the lights and ran into Casey's room, but he was not home yet. I checked the front door and it was locked. I searched the whole house and found that I was alone. I knew that what had happened was not my imagination, and yet, I couldn't explain it. I went back to my room, still pretty shook up, and fell on my knees and prayed for God to protect me. Finally I crawled back into bed, hugging my Bible as if it were a teddy bear, and this time I slept facing the door. It seemed like an eternity before the early morning rays finally came dancing through my window shades.

That morning I called Pastor Wilson and related my experience to him. As usual he was kind and compassionate and patiently waited until I had related the whole experience from beginning to end.

"Dan," he said calmly, "It appears that Satan is really

trying to throw a scare into you."

"Well," I replied honestly, "If that's what he was trying to do, then he succeeded!"

Then Pastor Wilson went on to explain to me that my Bible was not a magic book or a good luck charm. I couldn't sleep with it and hug it and expect it to protect me. If I wanted protection from the Word of God then that Word had to be inside of me, stored up in my heart and memory, ready to be used against Satan like a sword when he tried to attack me.

Then he said, "Dan, let me read you a passage from the book of Second Timothy, chapter one, verses six and seven: *And for this reason I remind you to kindle afresh the gift of God which is in you through the laying on of my hands. For God has not given us a Spirit of timidity, but of power and love and discipline.*"

"Dan, have you been praying to the Lord in tongues since we laid hands on you and you received the baptism in the Holy Spirit?" he asked.

"Well," I confessed, "No, I haven't. I tried praying in tongues a couple of times after that first experience, but it just sounded so silly to me that I thought I was just making it all up myself, so I quit."

"Dan, the devil would like to make us think that all scriptural things are silly, including our salvation experience. But even if the things of God do seem foolish to us, we need to do them anyway out of obedience to God and it will always bring about the best results for us. Even if praying in tongues does seem silly to you now, you need to discipline yourself to do it anyway because you are stirring up the gift of God that is within you and you receive power from God and a sound mind from God to know what to do when the devil tries to scare you as he has been doing."

Now this was all beginning to make a little sense to me.

"Dan," he continued, "Let me read you another passage of scripture found in Romans, chapter eight, verses twenty-six through twenty-eight: *And in the same way the Spirit also helps our weakness; for we do not know how* to pray as we should, but the Spirit Himself intercedes for us with groanings too deep for words; and He who searches the hearts knows what the mind of the Spirit is, because He intercedes for the saints according to the will of God. And we know that God causes all things to work together for good to those who love God, to those who are called according to His purpose."

"Dan, many times even older Christians get into situations in which they don't know how or what to pray for as they should. It's then that we pray in the Spirit's language and He helps our inabilities and causes everything to work out good for us," said Pastor Wilson.

"Dan, even though you were frightened by this experience you had with the devil, it has worked out for your good," he added.

"How do you figure that?" I questioned.

"Well," he answered, "from now on you should pray daily in your spiritual prayer language and you will receive more power, more love and your mind will become more disciplined to God's Word. If the devil tries to scare you again, you will be prepared with God's Word to defeat him."

"Now let me give you two more scripture verses in case you have another encounter with the devil like the last one. First, read James 4:7: *Submit therefore to God. Resist the devil and he will flee from you.* Then notice what Jesus said in Mark 16:17: 'And these signs will accompany those who have believed: in My name they will cast out demons . . .' "

I accepted Pastor Wilson's comforting advice, thanked him and hung up the telephone. Then I went to my room and got on my knees for a little conversation with my Heavenly Father.

"Heavenly Father," I said, "Please forgive me for neglecting to pray in the spiritual language You gave me, and forgive me for thinking it was silly too. Please help me to be a stronger and better Christian. In Jesus' name, amen." I knew instantly that the Lord had forgiven me because I had asked Him to.

I could sense the person of the Holy Spirit stirring deep within me and I began to speak in other tongues as the Spirit gave me utterance. I prayed for several minutes and I felt very lifted up on the inside. I felt more confident in the Lord and His presence was more real to me. Since that day I've made it a regular practice to get alone with my Heavenly Father and commune with Him in that heavenly language.

Several days later I was home alone again one evening. After watching television for a short period of time, I became sleepy and went to bed early. I woke up in the early morning hours to the most frightening experience that I've ever had. I had been sleeping on my stomach and I awoke with a thick, heavy, cold cloud upon me and that paralyzing fear held me motionless. I felt a great heavy weight upon my back and shoulders and my face was literally being shoved into my pillow. I was smothering. Someone or something was trying to kill me. I could barely turn my face enough to one side to gasp for a breath of air. In that same gasp I whispered the name, "Jesus, Jesus, Jesus." As I spoke that name the weight began to lift up off of me. Finally, I was able to turn over and sit up in bed.

At first I was terribly frightened. Then I began to think about all those scripture verses that Pastor Wilson had shared with me. I recognized this as the work of the devil again. My fear was turning to anger now. I was angry to think that the devil had the nerve to do such a thing to a child of God! I began to think out loud, "Satan, if you were a man I'd bust you in the mouth right now!"

As I sat there for a moment thinking about what had happened, a scripture passage came to mind that I had recently read in 2 Corinthians 10:3-6:

For though we walk in the flesh, we do not war according to the flesh,

for the weapons of our warfare are not of the flesh, but divinely powerful for the destruction of fortresses.

We are destroying speculations and every lofty thing raised up against the knowledge of God, and we are taking every thought captive to the obedience of Christ,

and we are ready to punish all disobedience, whenever your obedience is complete.

At that moment I realized that the Holy Spirit was

showing me that I could bust the devil in the mouth with the Word of God. I leaped out of bed and flipped on the lights. Then I boldly marched through the house to the front door and unlocked it. I flung the door wide open and turned to stare at the empty living room. With a loud voice I demanded: "Satan, in the name of the Lord Jesus Christ, I command you to get out of this house forever and don't you ever try to scare me again. Now get! In Jesus' name, amen!"

Then I slammed the door and marched victoriously back to my room. I began speaking in other tongues and the peace of God which passes all understanding began to flood my soul. I jumped back into bed and slept like a baby for the rest of the night. I've never had another scare like that one since then and the experience taught me that there truly is power over our unseen enemy in the name of our Lord Jesus Christ.

Not too long after that experience, Casey moved out of the apartment and moved back in with his parents. It seemed that the closer I became to the Lord the wider the gap grew between Casey and me. Victor was right. A house divided against itself cannot stand.

15

Many times in reading the Bible the Lord will make a verse of scripture so real to you that you just know in your heart that He is speaking directly to you. This happened to me the very first time I remember reading Numbers 23:19: *"God is not a man, that He should lie, nor a son of man, that He should repent; has He said, and will He not do it? Or has He spoken, and will He not make it good?"*

What this verse was saying to my heart was that the Bible, from cover to cover, truly is God's revelation of Himself to all mankind and that throughout this book our Heavenly Father says what He means and means what He says! I became excited when I thought that everything in the Bible was the truth because it is impossible for God to tell a lie. As Paul puts it in Romans 3:4: *"Let God be found true, and every man be found a liar."* Men tell lies for various reasons, but God never has and never will tell us a lie. His Word is forever settled.

This experience caused me to want to study the Bible more fervently to find out more about God and more about myself. Then I ran across 2 Timothy 3:16-17: *All Scripture is inspired by God and profitable for teaching, for reproof, for correction, for training in righteousness; that the man of God may be adequate, equipped for every good work.*

This confirmed to me even more that the Bible was God-inspired and trustworthy. It seemed to kindle a fire in my heart to want to learn more about God. But my biggest problem at that time was the fact that I really didn't like to read. It was hard for me to discipline myself to sit down and read for very long. Then I came across Romans 10:17: *So faith comes from hearing, and hearing by the word of Christ.* This passage sparked within me the idea that perhaps I could buy the Bible on cassette tapes and listen to the Word instead of reading it. This way I would be "hearing" the Word of Christ and increasing my faith.

I looked into this idea more thoroughly and found out that if I were to get the Old Testament and New Testament on cassette tapes plus a nice stereo tape player to play them on, it would cost me about five hundred dollars.

Well, I didn't have that much money and I didn't know where I could get it. I prayed and asked my Heavenly Father where I could get five hundred dollars, but I received no immediate answer.

Then somehow, a few days later, I came across a book written by Oral Roberts entitled *Miracle of Seed Faith*. I read the book thoroughly and received what appeared to be some good sound Biblical advice. The message of the book seemed to be based primarily on one verse, Luke 6:38: *"Give, and it will be given to you: good measure, pressed down, shaken together, running over, they will pour into your lap. For by your standard of measure it will be measured to you in return."*

Brother Roberts stated that when Christians have needs, they should make their needs "seeds" and plant them in the Kingdom of God. He said that God will cause our seeds to grow into an abundant harvest so that all our needs will be met and we will have enough left over to share with other needy people. It was simply the process of sowing and reaping, and it always works.

This seemed to agree with what I had recently read in Malachi 3:8-10:

"Will a man rob God? Yet you are robbing Me! But you say, 'How have we robbed Thee?' In tithes and offerings.

"You are cursed with a curse, for you are robbing Me, the whole nation of you!

"Bring the whole tithe into the storehouse, so that there may be food in My house, and test Me now in this," says the Lord of hosts, *"if I will not open for you the windows of heaven and pour out for you a blessing until it overflows."*

After reading this I realized why I had so many needs. I wasn't planting any seeds. I was robbing God of the opportunity to bless me because I wasn't giving tithes of all that He had blessed me with. I knew once again that the Lord was trying to show me truth through His Word. I immediately asked Him to forgive me and began to give tithes of all that I had. Not just money, but my time and my talents. Then the blessings began to flow.

I read Matthew 18:19 and decided to act upon it to see if it really would work for me: *"Again I say to you, that if two of you agree on earth about anything that they may ask, it shall be done for them by My Father who is in heaven."* At the next church service I went forward to the altar for prayer. I asked the pastor if he would agree with me in prayer about a financial need I had. I put five dollars in the offering plate as a seed and we asked the Lord to multiply it back to me one hundred times so I could have five hundred dollars to buy my stereo and Bible tapes.

From that day on I thanked the Lord for answering that prayer. About three weeks later a man whom I didn't even know came to me and gave me a certified check for five hundred dollars. I joyfully accepted it as my miracle from the Lord and I bought my stereo and Bible tapes.

Ever since that experience I have always planted seeds and the Lord always meets my needs and more. I've learned since then that the Lord not only wants to supply my financial and material needs, but also my physical and spiritual requests as well. Jesus said in John 16:24: *"Until now you have asked for nothing in My name; ask and you will receive, that your joy may be made full."* My joy is at its fullest when my needs are supplied and my prayers are answered.

My mother had gone to church most of her life but deep down in my heart I doubted that she had ever really been born again. I had learned that going to church does not make a person a Christian any more than going to the movies makes him an actor. Each individual must have a personal encounter with the Lord Jesus Christ and be born again. I began to talk to my mother about this and it seemed to irritate her, especially coming from me. She even said that I was going overboard and becoming fanatical. All I knew to do was to turn her over to the Lord in prayer. I prayed, "Heavenly Father, please let Mom have a real born-again experience and fill her with the Holy Ghost. In Jesus' name, amen." Then I began to thank Him for the answer.

Shortly after that, my mother rededicated her life to the Lord and had a born-again experience. Then on the World Day of Prayer in 1976 she was home alone praying, "Jesus, if this experience called the baptism in the Holy

Ghost is real and a valid experience for Christians today, then please baptize me in the Holy Spirit now, amen."

When we ask in simple child-like faith believing, we always receive. The Lord filled her with the Holy Spirit as she knelt on the living room floor and she began to speak in other tongues as the Holy Spirit gave the utterance. What an exciting telephone call I received from her that day.

Soon after that she left the little church where she had been attending because her spirit was not being fed God's Word there. She began attending services at the Full Gospel church in Clarksburg where I was attending. What a thrill it was to watch her grow spiritually since she made Jesus the Lord of her life.

On Good Friday of that same year, I took the day off from work to attend a Good Friday Morning Prayer Breakfast. My mother attended the meeting with me and after the service had concluded I drove her the fifteen miles back to Salem. On the return trip to Clarksburg I was driving along and praising the Lord in other tongues. I noticed an elderly gentleman standing along the road trying to hitch a ride. I felt compassion for him and stopped to offer him a ride. He was poorly dressed and looked quite weather beaten. I noticed as he got in the car that he was crippled and walked with a crutch. As we drove along I began to question him about his background.

"About six years ago I was involved in an accident at the steel mill where I worked," he told me. "I broke my hip and it never healed correctly. I've walked bent over and with this crutch ever since."

"Where are you headed now?" I asked him.

"I've been hitch-hiking for two days now trying to make it home to my wife and children," he replied. "They live about ninety miles from here. I don't have any money and I haven't eaten for two days. I stopped in Salem at one of the churches to see if they would help me out a little."

"Praise the Lord," I replied, "what happened?"

"The preacher told me that his church didn't have any funds to help people like me and he shut the door in my face."

I was really pricked in my heart when he told me that. "The God I serve will not treat you like that, Mister," I told him.

Then I began to share with him my testimony of how Jesus was changing my life. He became quite upset.

"Sonny, I used to go to church for years, but I never got anything out of it."

I knew instantly that he had backslidden because he had not trusted the Lord and continued to feed on God's Word. Jesus said in Matthew 4:4: *"It is written, 'Man shall not live by bread alone, but on every word that proceeds out of the mouth of God.'"* Just as the physical man needs food daily to stay healthy and survive, our spiritual man needs food daily from God's Word to survive the trials and temptations of this life.

As we continued to drive along I offered to take him to the Greyhound Bus terminal and buy him a bus ticket to his home and see that he got a good hot meal.

"I don't want your charity, son," he resisted. "Just take me to the next entrance ramp to the interstate highway and I'll get out of your car."

The remainder of the drive was in silence. As we approached the ramp I remembered that there was a restaurant just ahead so I passed by the ramp and drove into the restaurant parking lot. I figured that at this point his hunger was probably greater than his pride. He humbly thanked me for the ride and for the money I handed him.

"Mister, would it be alright with you if I said a little prayer before you get out of the car?" I asked him.

"Go ahead, son," he said as he bowed his head.

I was very nervous and didn't know what to pray except in my heart I felt so sorry for this poor soul. I took his hand in mine and placed my right hand on his forehead and simply said, "Heavenly Father, please show this man that You still love him; and in the name of the Lord Jesus Christ, be healed!"

As I removed my hand from his forehead I was startled by a noise that sounded like a bone breaking. The old man's body straightened out in the front seat of my car and he began to cry. I became a little frightened at the sight. I looked in amazement as he opened the car door and stood up straight in the parking lot. He picked up his crutch and threw it down on the pavement. He walked and danced around the parking lot with not a trace of even a limp. The Lord had given him a miracle and he was divinely healed. I was at a loss for words as I got out of the car to observe this miracle. This was the first time I had ever personally witnessed an actual miracle take place. We lifted our hands and thanked God for the wonderful thing He had done.

I was so excited when I got home that I ran to my room and fell on my knees and began praying in tongues. After praying for a long time I became silent and just waited on the Lord. I sensed that the Spirit of the Lord was going to speak to me. A verse of scripture seemed to pop into my mind. It was Mark 16:17-18:

"And these signs will accompany those who have believed: in My name...

"they will lay hands on the sick, and they will recover."

This was what I had just experienced. Then the Lord led me to pick up my Bible and I read in Acts about a similar experience that the Apostles Peter and John had had with a lame man. After the Lord had healed the man, the people ran together to question the apostles about what had taken place. In Acts 3:12-16 Peter answers them:

"Men of Israel, why do you marvel at this, or why do you gaze at us, as if by our own power or piety we had made him walk?

"The God of Abraham, Isaac, and Jacob, the God of our fathers, has glorified His servant Jesus, the one whom you delivered up, and disowned in the presence of Pilate, when he had decided to release Him.

"But you disowned the Holy and Righteous One, and asked for a murderer to be granted to you,

"but put to death the Prince of life, the one whom God raised from the dead, a fact to which we are witnesses.

"And on the basis of faith in His name, it is the name of Jesus which has strengthened this man whom you see and know; and the faith which comes through Him has given him this *perfect health in the presence of you all.''*

The Lord was showing me that the man I had prayed for was healed by my faith in the name of Jesus, and not by any power or holiness of my own. This experience greatly increased my faith to pray for other sick people. Since that time I have prayed and watched the Lord open deaf ears and give sight to the blind. I've seen Him heal crippled and diseased people of all kinds by a simple prayer offered in faith in Jesus' name. I don't always understand the ways of the Lord, but I always trust Him. He has healed my physical body many times and once miraculously kept me from having to undergo major surgery. All of these experiences have strengthened my faith and caused me to agree with the writer of Hebrews: *Jesus Christ is the same yesterday and today, yes and forever* (Heb. 13:8).

16

All of my life I had enjoyed making new friends and getting to know different people. Since I had become a Christian, I noticed that I didn't have too much in common any more with most of my life-long friends. I still loved them and prayed sincerely for them, but I could see that the things they were doing for happiness and fun were only leading them to unhappiness and separation from God. I tried to explain these things to them but for the most part, they weren't interested.

The Lord began to give me a whole new circle of friends. They weren't only friends but real brothers and sisters in the family of God who genuinely cared about my happiness. Through these friends I began to experience the real warmth and sincere love of our Heavenly Father. This was the kind of love my heart had always searched for.

After Nina had broken off our relationship I didn't desire to get involved with another girl any time soon. I had been on a couple of dates in the past few months but the girls were not Christian girls and our dates didn't amount to much. I had two favorite subjects I liked to discuss, Jesus and Nina, and neither of the two seemed to make a hit with any of my dates.

Then through some mutual friends I learned that Dorlene had moved back home from Florida. Dorlene and I were very close before I had ever met Nina. Now that she was back in West Virginia I became excited at the thought of seeing her again. I thought that perhaps I could persuade her to be born again and we would serve the Lord together. I got on the telephone immediately and called her mother's house. Dorlene answered the phone and seemed sincerely happy to hear from me. We made a date to go out to dinner that evening.

It was really good to see her again and after a delightful dinner we went to my house to relax and talk. As soon as we got relaxed in the living room, Dorlene decided she wanted to get high. "Hey Dan, why don't you roll us up a joint and we'll catch a little buzz," she remarked. Now I was faced with a real moment of truth in my life. I had to be honest!

"Dorlene," I said slowly, "some things have changed while you were in Florida."

"Oh, what things?" she questioned.

"Well, I don't smoke pot or use drugs or drink alcohol or do a lot of things we used to do together," I answered.

"Well, Dan ole boy, what brought about all these major changes?" she asked.

"Dorlene, while you were in Florida, I accepted Jesus Christ as my personal Lord and Savior," I said.

"That's cool man, but what's Jesus got against having a little fun?"

"Honey, Jesus doesn't have anything against people having fun. In fact, He wants people to be happy. But those things we did didn't bring lasting happiness and you know it. I've learned from personal experience that only Jesus can give you lasting happiness, peace of mind and satisfaction in life," I said. The room became quiet as she pondered what I had said.

"Dorlene, why don't you just give Jesus a chance and I promise you'll never be sorry you did. I'll help you all I can and we'll have fun learning and growing together," I said. There was another pause of silence. I was nervous and I could tell she was growing uneasy too.

"Dan, I'm really happy for you and I hope everything works out okay for you. But I'm just not ready to make that decision. When it's my time, I'll know. I gotta get my own head on straight before I can think about God. Thanks, but no thanks," was her final reply.

I didn't know how to tell her that Jesus was the only one who could ever put her head on straight. So many people live under the misunderstanding that they must work something out and then come to the Lord. Or they think that God has appointed some day down the road for them to get saved. The only day God ever appointed for anyone to get saved is today. The Lord said in 2 Corinthians 6:2 "At the acceptable time I listened to you, and on the day of salvation I helped you;" behold, now is "the acceptable time," behold, now is "the day of salvation." If you are not saved, then today is the day you should surrender your life to the Lord Jesus Christ!

My heart sank as I saw my plans for Dorlene and me suddenly fade away.

"Danny, can you please take me home now," she asked.

"Sure," I replied.

It was a quiet ride to her mother's house. I stopped the car in front of the house and our eyes met for a few fleeting seconds then she looked out into the night.

"Well thanks for everything and I wish you the best of luck in what you're doing," she said.

"Hey, you're welcome and remember I'll be praying for you," I said as I leaned over to kiss her on the cheek.

"Bye-bye," we said.

I didn't hear from Dorlene for several weeks, but she had been on my mind. I had been working at the factory all day and was hurrying to get to night school on time. I was glancing over the evening paper and walking towards the front door. Suddenly, I stopped in my tracks. My hands became cold and my heart grew numb as I looked into that newspaper and saw Dorlene's name listed in the obituary column. My mind refused to accept the facts that were before my eyes. I threw the paper down and ran to the telephone knowing that this just couldn't be true. I dialed Dorlene's number and waited as it rang. Finally her mother answered the telephone. It was true. Her mother explained to me that Dorlene had left the house with some friends the night before. They were all using drugs that night and Dorlene had accidently overdosed. She died in the emergency room while they were pumping her stomach. It was too late. The drug was in her blood stream and had done its fatal work.

Dorlene's mother asked if I would be a pall bearer at the funeral and I agreed. As I hung up the telephone I felt weak and helpless. Death is often too real to cope with. The next evening I was the first person to arrive at the funeral home. I slowly approached the casket and stood there alone. My thoughts began to drift back to the time we had raced hand and hand, barefoot in the sand, across the beach in North Carolina. Life is so carefree when you're in love. At this timeless moment I found myself asking the question, "What is love?" A silent pause held no answer. Then deep within me a gentle voice seemed to whisper, "God is love, and any relationship outside of Him and away from His protective hand is in danger of ending in tragedy."

I looked down into Dorlene's lifeless face. She was beautiful. I remembered her long dark hair blowing in the wind and the sparkle of her big brown eyes. We had our differences of opinions but we always seemed to work things out. I recalled the first time we had met. My memory recalled every detail of our relationship up to this very moment. Tears welled up in my eyes as I reached down to hold her cold hand and stroke her beautiful hair. "Why Jesus, why did this have to happen," I cried. But this time I received no answer. Only a long empty silence. I walked away thinking that only God really knows what happens from this point on. I spent a sleepless night crying and praying and dreading the funeral service the next day.

The next morning it was raining and dreary outside. I went to the funeral home and tried as best as I could to be of some comfort to Dorlene's family. When the day had ended I cherished the time that I could finally be alone with my Heavenly Father. I escaped to my room and fell prostrate on the floor and began to sob uncontrollably before the Lord. "Why, why, why?" I begged to know the answer. I prayed in tongues for what seemed hours until I was exhausted. I lay silently and lost all track of time. Then the Word of God came. The words from the book of John, chapter ten and verse ten, echoed and echoed from the chambers of my heart: *"The thief comes only to steal, and kill, and destroy; I came that they might have life, and might have it abundantly."*

The Spirit of the Lord was showing me through God's Word that the devil, Satan, is the thief. And he is the one responsible for stealing and killing and destroying people's lives. Jesus Christ came into the world to give people abundant life if they would only believe on Him and trust their lives into His hands.

The Lord was showing me that the devil uses drugs, alcohol, illicit sex or anything else that appeals to the desires of man to lure him away from receiving real life through Jesus Christ. Approximately 206,000 people die daily all over the world. Many of them have refused the Gospel message of the Lord Jesus Christ. Millions have died and their lives have been destroyed by the devil because their eyes have been blinded and their ears have been closed to the saving, healing, and delivering power of Jesus Christ. They blame God for all their troubles when in reality it's the devil who has stolen and destroyed their lives.

When I realized this truth I became angry at what the devil had done and was doing to all mankind. I cried out to God, "Father, what can I do to help stop the devil?" Again a scripture verse came to mind, this time from 2 Timothy 2:15: *Be diligent to present yourself approved to God as a workman who does not need to be ashamed, handling accurately the word of truth.* The Lord was showing me that He would use me to help other people, but I must first study to show myself approved unto Him and be able to correctly share His truth with others.

Many people, young and old alike, had lost their lives like Dorlene because they didn't know or wouldn't accept the facts about Jesus Christ. I arose from my bedroom floor with a deeper desire to know God and His Word. I made up my mind that with God's help and by His grace I would tell the whole world about Jesus Christ. It was too late for me to help Dorlene now, but it was not too late to prevent others from having their lives stolen, killed and destroyed by the devil.

17

The local church I was attending was very active in supporting missionary work. The whole world had been shocked by the tragic event which took place in the small Central American country of Guatemala on February 4, 1976. An earthquake had literally devastated the country and left thousands homeless and multiplied thousands had lost their lives. They needed immediate relief. Our congregation was informed of a ministry in McAllen, Texas, called Frontline Mininstries that was sending supplies and volunteers to Guatemala to help the people recover from this great tragedy and to proclaim the Gospel of Jesus Christ.

The founder and director of Frontline Ministries, Harold Dunn, was in Clarksburg to encourage the area churches to get involved in this missionary outreach. Not only could a church donate money and supplies to help in this emergency, but Harold was encouraging members of the local churches to donate two weeks of their time and go to Guatemala to actually participate in the missionary work. The whole idea was revolutionary and sounded very exciting. I always wondered what it would be like to go to a foreign country and be a missionary. This seemed like an ideal opportunity to find out. However, there was a slight problem. I didn't have any extra money and I knew this trip would be rather expensive.

The only thing I knew to do was to go to the Lord in earnest prayer and tell him all about my desire. After presenting my request to my Heavenly Father, I stayed on my knees and remained silent before the Lord. The Holy Spirit brought to me the Word of the Lord and I received comfort and encouragment in the thirty-seventh Psalm, verses three through five:

Trust in the Lord, and do good; dwell in the land and cultivate faithfulness.

Delight yourself in the Lord; and He will give you the desires of your heart.

Commit your way to the Lord, trust also in Him, and He will do it.

I knew in my heart that the Lord was speaking to me through this passage of scripture and I knew He would work something out. I shared my desire with my pastor, and he said he would pray also. It wasn't long before the good news came. The church was willing to send me on a two-week missionary journey and pay all the expenses.

"Praise the Lord!" I shouted.

The church had agreed to send Pastor Wilson too. Immediately we began making preparations to embark on our first missionary journey. My employer granted me two weeks' vacation and on August 2, 1976, we boarded our plane in Clarksburg, West Virginia. We arrived that evening at the Miami Airport and a car transported us to the Miami Airport Inn. We met with thirty-four other Christians from all over the United States who would make up this Frontline Ministries Team on a mission of good will into Guatemala, Central America.

We all met together that evening in Room 239 for prayer, worship, fellowship and to discuss the details of our trip. It was evident that the Spirit of the Lord was present in that room as we worshipped together. After receiving instructions from our team leaders we returned to our rooms. Pastor Wilson and I prayed together about the trip and went to bed around midnight.

Around 2:00 a.m., I was awakened and sensed the presence of the Holy Spirit as a thick cloud in the room. The words "Isaiah 61" kept ringing over and over in my mind until finally I drifted back into a peaceful sleep. I was awakened at 6:00 by the alarm clock and immediately arose and reached for my Bible.

I turned to the sixty-first chapter of the book of Isaiah and the first four verses seemed to leap up off the page at me:

The spirit of the Lord God is upon me, because the Lord has anointed me to bring good news to the afflicted; He has sent me to bind up the brokenhearted, to proclaim liberty to captives, and freedom to prisoners;

To proclaim the favorable year of the Lord, and the day of vengeance of our God; to comfort all who mourn, to grant those who mourn in Zion, giving them a garland instead of ashes, the oil of gladness instead of mourning, the mantle of praise instead of a spirit of fainting. So they will be called oaks of righteousness, the planting of the Lord, that He may be glorified.

Then they will rebuild the ancient ruins, they will raise up the former devastations, and they will repair the ruined cities, the desolations of many generations.

I knew that this was the Lord's way of telling me what we would be doing for the next two weeks in Guatemala. Our plane left Miami Airport at 9:50 a.m. Florida time and we were asked to set our watches back to 7:50 a.m. Guatemala time. After we ate breakfast, our plane landed im Managua, Nicaragua, for a thirty-minute layover. It was exciting for me to watch all the people rushing around the terminal and speaking in Spanish. I couldn't speak any Spanish, so I just stood still and smiled at everybody as they rushed by. We were not allowed outside the airport terminal building. There were soldiers with rifles posted at every exit.

I felt a little more relaxed when we were back on our airplane. The flight was enjoyable and we landed in Guatemala City around noon. Our group stood together in the outside airport lobby and sang choruses while we waited for our luggage and transportation. We were to be transported about 25 miles outside of Guatemala City near the jungle. We would be staying at an old abandoned chicken farm located at the base of a volcano. Our job would be to renovate this ranch and turn it into an orphanage for the children who lost their parents in the earthquake.

The vans arrived and we were on our way. The scenery outside the city was breathtakingly beautiful. Although the earthquake had occured six months ago, the damage that it had caused was still visible. However, the natural beauty of the country remained untouched. When we arrived at the farm it was raining. The people there told us that it was their rainy season and we could expect rain for the next two weeks. We knew that if it did rain every day, the progress of our work would be greatly hindered. As Christians we had learned to completely trust our lord Jesus Christ and not be discouraged by our circumstances.

We all joined hands together in a big circle and asked the Lord to stop the rain in order for us to accomplish the work that He had sent us there to do. We got unpacked, had our evening meal and went to bed.

We arose early the next morning to work and the sun was shining brightly. We experienced no more rain until the day we boarded our plane for the trip home. The natives were perplexed. They had never seen anything like this before.

This was only the first of many miracles that the Lord performed while this Frontline Ministry Team worked together to build the orphanage. The Lord miraculously purified our drinking water and kept us all completely healthy during our visit there. The presence of the Lord was very evident in our camp.

There were already eight orphan children living on the farm and many more were waiting to come when we would complete our work. We were there to rebuild the ancient ruins, raise up former desolations, repair the wasted cities and preach the acceptable year of our Lord, just as the Lord had shown me. Our Frontline Ministry Team was made up of pastors, carpenters, plumbers, electricians, bricklayers, manual laborers and ladies who cooked and washed our clothes. We started our days with prayer and ended with prayer and the Lord greatly blessed all of the work that was done in between.

On Sunday, August 8, 1976, we held our morning worship service at 8:00 a.m. We then boarded some vehicles that would take us into Guatemala City to visit the earthquake victims. Our first stop was a camp named "February Fourth," so named because the earthquake had occurred on that particular date. Most of us had never seen a situation like the one unfolding before our eyes. "February Fourth" was a camp to which earthquake victims had migrated. The area covered about one square mile of ground and the population was growing to nearly 50 thousand migrants despite the death and disease that plagued it. We were informed that an average of two children died every day and at least one person would commit suicide each day. There were open sewers, no running water and not much food. People were living on the bare ground with only tin and sticks and pieces of plastic tied together for shelter. I saw children living in cardboard boxes. These people had lost everything including most of their families in the earthquake. I had never seen anything like it in my life.

My thoughts returned to my home and how good life was in the United States as compared to this scene. We are a very blessed people in the United States. I thought of the scripture found in the thirty-third Psalm, verse twelve: *Blessed is the nation whose God is the Lord, the people whom He has chosen for His own inheritance.* I believe that the United States is a blessed nation, because of our faith in Jesus Christ. But, today many people have lost that faith and our nation is greatly suffering because of it. If we are to remain a blessed nation and a great world power, we need a spiritual revival and a return to a basic child-like trust in Jesus Christ as the Savior of the world!

As I looked upon this suffering humanity I realized that these people not only needed food and shelter, but they also needed to hear the Gospel message of our Lord Jesus Christ. He is the only one who can save and sustain their lives. We left "February Fourth" and went on to another camp called "Zone Seven" where other Frontline Ministry Teams had been to work and preach the Gospel. The atmosphere was different. We were warmly greeted by children who were ready to sing choruses and praise the Lord together with us. We were invited to return to "Zone Seven" on Tuesday evening to hold church services.

Tuesday evening was an exciting time. The people all crowded around us. Pastor Wilson and other pastors preached the Gospel through the help of an interpreter. We were able to pray for the people and to give them Bibles to read. It was a glorious experience to see them accept Jesus.

We worked diligently together the remainder of our days there to complete the work of finishing the orphanage. It was hard work, but worth the effort. We finished everything but a few minor details before the scheduled time we were to leave. The Lord truly blessed our labors.

Our last evening together was a memorable occasion. We visited a local restaurant and enjoyed a steak and shrimp dinner together. After dinner, the restaurant owner was kind enough to allow us to hold services outside around his swimming pool. The power of the Holy Spirit fell upon us as we worshipped and praised the Lord. We even had a water baptismal service in the swimming pool. Many of us stayed up most of the night just to fellowship and talk about the things of God. The next morning we packed our belongings and prepared for our return home. We shared morning devotions together. It was a special time. In just two weeks our hearts had been knit together forever by the love of God and the person of the Holy Spirit. We had seen the hand of the living God move mightily on our behalf as we performed His work in Guatemala. Now it was time to return home and share our experiences with our local congregations.

We took some group pictures, then everybody loaded onto the vehicles that would transport us to the airport in Guatemala City. We boarded our plane at 3:30 p.m. Guatemala time and landed at 10:00 p.m. in Miami, Florida. We sang psalms and hymns and spiritual songs and made melody in our hearts to the Lord all during the return flight. Pastor Wilson and I had to spend the night in Miami in order to catch our flight home at 7:10 a.m. the next morning. We arrived in Clarksburg, West Virginia, at 1:15 p.m. and were warmly greeted by our families and members of the church.

As I rode home that afternoon with my mother, I closed my eyes and my mind reviewed all that had taken place in the past two weeks. I thanked my Heavenly Father for every emotion, experience, encounter and person that I had the priviledge to come in contact with on this exciting missionary journey. I came home with a whole new idea of Christianity. I had a burning desire in my heart to share the love of Jesus Christ with everybody. I prayed and asked the Lord to allow me to travel more and spread His Gospel message.

Since that first missionary journey there have been many others from Clarksburg who have taken two-week missionary journeys through the ministry of Harold Dunn and Frontline Ministries.

18

After returning home from such an exciting missionary journey I found myself becoming bolder to share the Gospel message with the people with whom I worked at the factory. I had seen and experienced the Lord working in such marvelous ways that I wanted to tell everybody about it. I began to notice that I was talking to my fellow employees about the Lord more than I was doing the job that I was being paid to do. I believe the Holy Spirit showed me that by doing this, I was not setting a very good example of what a Christian should be. I was being paid for eight hours of labor a day. I asked the Lord to forgive me for my mistake and to show me how I could be a good witness for Him and still give my employer a full day's work.

While I was praying, the Lord showed me that I would be a good witness by doing a good day's work and simple allowing my life-style to be an example to those around me. I decided that rather than talking individually to my fellow employees on my employer's time, I would write a personal letter to each of them on my own time and tell them of the happiness I had found through Jesus Christ.

The following is a copy of the letter dated October 1, 1976, which I mailed to every employee with whom I worked at Lockheed-Georgia Company, Clarksburg Plant:

Dear Fellow Employee:

I'd just like to take a few minutes of your time to share with you something exciting that happened to me. First, I would like to ask you a couple of questions. Are you ''fully'' satisfied with your life? Have you ever wished you could just quit and start all over again?

For the first twenty-two years of my life, I tried everything I knew of to make myself happy. Wine, women and song used to make me happy. But only for a while. I could never be satisfied with just one woman, one wine or one song. Know what I mean?

Less than two years ago, I accepted Jesus Christ as my Savior. Now I'm not writing to try to push any church, denomination or religion on you. I just want to share what happened to me. I wanted to start my life all over again because I was not satisfied.

Read in your Bible John 3:3-7 where Jesus said, **"You must be born again."** I never liked to go to church very much because I thought all those people were hypocrites. But the Apostle Paul said in 2 Corinthians 5:17: **Therefore if any man is in Christ, he is a new creature; the old things passed away; behold, new things have come.** You may already be a Christian, but can't seem to muster enough power to overcome temptation and old habits. Jesus Christ has that power for you. Read about it in chapters one and two of the book of Acts. The power that came down on the day of Pentecost is also available to you today.

Hebrews 13:8 says: **Jesus Christ is the same yesterday and today, yes and forever.** You may not want to take my word for it. So pray and ask Jesus about it. He will never lie to you.

In the office lounge is a free magazine called **Voice** placed there by the Full Gospel Businessmen's Fellowship International. This magazine is full of testimonies from people who have experienced the same new life that I have. Please pick up your free copy on your lunch break. I only want you to be as happy as I am.

Your friend,
Dan Nicholson

After mailing a copy of this letter to every individual in the plant, it was no longer necessary for me to look for people to talk to about the Lord. They came to me. My lunch hour and break times became counseling sessions. It was exciting to see how the Lord was using that letter. Over a period of the next few months, several of my fellow employees were actually born again as a result. This inspired me to want to do more for my Lord. I spent most of my spare time studying the Bible.

Sometimes I would walk the city streets and hand out Gospel tracts and literature to people. I wanted everybody to personally know Jesus. I even went to a big rock concert being held in Clarksburg and stood outside the door and handed out Gospel tracts to everybody who was going inside. Some of my old friends saw me there and they thought I had gone crazy. I only wanted to do all I possibly could to share the love of Jesus Christ with the unsaved people. But it seemed like the more I tried to do, the more I wanted to do, and yet an inner voice was telling me to rest. But I didn't know how to rest in the Lord.

I began to strongly sense that the Lord was calling me into full-time ministry. But I didn't know what to do about it. I was attending church services and home Bible studies and prayer meetings, and people began encouraging me to enter the ministry. People who were endowed by God with the gift of prophecy would lay hands on me and say things like, "Thus saith the Lord, I have called you to proclaim My Word, but rest in Me and I will direct your steps." The only problem was, I didn't know how to rest. Was I supposed to go to Bible school? If not, what was I supposed to do? My mind was filled with confusion. I had the attitude that resting meant doing nothing, and if I did nothing, people would think I was lazy. I struggled with this thing so much that I actually began to feel lazy, guilty and condemned. I felt I was losing the peace of God. Something was wrong.

This was a spiritual battle and I cried out to God for help. Once again the Word of God became real to me from the book of Romans, chapter eight and verse one: *There is therefore now no condemnation for those who are in Christ Jesus.* I knew that the Lord was not making me feel lazy, guilty and condemned. It was the devil making me feel that way. The peace of God returned to me and I prayed and asked the Lord to teach me what it meant to rest in Him.

Shortly thereafter a guest evangelist came to our local church. Strangely enough, he preached on the subject of resting in the Lord. I picked up a couple of good points from his sermon. He said that being a Christian was really not our responsibility, but rather it was our "response ability"— our response to God's ability. He said that we Christians need to learn to quit worrying and fretting ourselves and simply learn to respond to the ability of God who lives within us. That seemed to go right along with what the Bible says in Philippians 2:13: *For it is God who is at work in you, both to will and to work for His pleasure.*

The evangelist quoted from Matthew 5:14-16 where Jesus told His disciples:

"You are the light of the world. A city set on a hill cannot be hidden."

"Neither do men light a lamp, and put it under the peck-measure, but on the lampstand; and it gives light to all who are in the house."

"Let your light shine before men in such a way that they may see your good works, and glorify your Father who is in Heaven."

Then the evangelist pointed to the lights which were hanging from the church ceiling. He said, "See how these lights are bringing light to this whole room? And yet they are not making any noise. If we as Christians would allow the love of Jesus Christ to shine through us, then we wouldn't have to make any noise either. For people couldn't help but see our shining example and know that God was living in us. We should all just shine and rest in Him."

I tossed these thoughts over and over in my mind for several days and asked the Lord to help me understand more clearly what it meant to rest in Him.

One evening I was studying the seventeenth chapter of 1 Kings. I was really impressed by the way the Lord had taken care of Elijah the prophet. Elijah had hidden himself by the brook of Cherith as the Lord had directed him. While Elijah rested and waited for further instructions, the Lord commanded the ravens to feed him with bread and meat twice a day and he drank fresh water from the brook. I went to bed that night thinking what a wonderful God I serve. He always takes care of us and He is full of marvelous surprises.

I arose the next morning to go to work and found that a heavy snow had fallen during the night. When I went outside I found that my car was blocked in my parking space. I couldn't back up because of the snow and I couldn't move forward because a car was parked too close if front of me. I became somewhat disgusted. I went back to my apartment and phoned my boss to inform him that I couldn't make it out to work that morning. Then I decided to go back to bed and just forget about my problems. But before I went to bed I knelt to pray: "Heavenly Father, I'm sorry I got disgusted this morning. But it seems like I'm getting pressure from all sides and I can't handle it. I'm trying to rest, but I don't clearly understand it. Please take all these problems. In Jesus' name. I'm going to bed, amen."

After I had been asleep for an hour or so, I was awakened by the sound of an automobile engine starting. I got up and looked out my window. The car that had been parked in front of me had moved and I was no longer blocked in. As I stood gazing out the window, the Spirit of the Lord began to speak inside of me: "My son, this is what I mean by rest. If you will give Me all of your problems as you did this one and then relax, I will remove all obstacles from your path as this one was removed. Only commit the obstacle to Me, trust Me and rest in Me."

Suddenly I became excited. I had received a definite understanding of what it meant to rest in the Lord. I knew now that the Lord meant exactly what He said in 1 Peter 5:7: *Casting all your anxiety upon Him, because He cares for you.*

I made up my mind then and there that I was going to cast literally *all* my cares upon the Lord and let Him work out the details of my life. After all, that's what He said He wants us all to do. So once again I decided to take God at His Word, and it works.

I got dressed again and drove to Salem to spend the day with my mother and tell her all about this experience. Later that evening I returned home for still another surprise. As I walked into my apartment I saw a big black bird sitting in the middle of my bed. I was startled and the first thing I did was say, "Lord, is that You?" The black bird began to fly around the room and landed in the floor by the kitchen door and then just looked at me. I opened the door and the bird hopped outside, looked at me again, and then flew away. This was all very puzzling to me so I went back inside and began to pray and ask the Lord what it all meant.

After praying awhile and waiting on the Lord I began

to discern the voice of the Lord speaking to me from deep within: "My son, do you remember reading last night about Elijah, My prophet, and how I separated him and sent the ravens to feed him bread and flesh?"

"Yes, Lord, I remember," I said.

"I desire to separate you and feed you with My Word. I will guide you and instruct you in all your ways. Only be a doer of My Word and not merely a hearer."

Then the Lord directed me to my Bible and I read the passage found in the book of 1 John, chapter two, verse twenty-seven: *And as for you, the anointing which you received from Him abides in you, and you have no need for anyone to teach you; but as His anointing teaches you about all things, and is true and is not a lie, and just as it has taught you, you abide in Him.*

Again I knew the Lord was showing me the importance of daily studying His Word and applying it to my life. I made the decision that I would not go away to a Bible school. The local church that I was attending offered a four-year course of study on the Bible and ministry. I became a member of the church and enrolled in the courses offered. This also gave me the opportunity to apply what I was learning in the local congregation. I was becoming more and more excited at how the Lord was answering my prayers and directing my life.

19

Christian Communication Center (Channel 46), located in Clarksburg, West Virginia, is a ministry founded by Joe Rose. Joe believed that God had called him to spread the Gospel of Jesus Christ via television throughout West Virginia and to provide the state with wholesome family television programming. Many area Christians donate not only their money, but also their time and talents to help suport this ministry. People with various needs call in daily and volunteer prayer counselors pray with them on the telephone and the Lord answers their prayers. Many interesting Bible teachers and evangelists pass through the Clarksburg area and stop in at Christian Communications Center to teach and preach on that channel.

On one particular day, as I was working as a telephone counselor, I had the privilege of meeting an evangelist from South Africa named Robert Thom. He was known universally for his prophetic ministry and was sometimes referred to as "Africa's Man of Faith." It was very exciting to listen to him tell of his travels around the world and of spreading the Gospel message of our Lord Jesus Christ. Soon our meeting became a prayer meeting as Brother Thom began to pray individually for everybody in the room. When he came to me, he laid both his hands upon my head and began to speak: "And you shall be blessed mightily with the gifts of healing and the gift of miracles and the word of knowledge shall work mightily in you." His resonant voice rang in my ears as I sat in wonder at what this all meant.

Joe Rose invited me to have dinner with him and Robert Thom that evening. We ate at the airport restaurant, because Brother Thom had to catch a plane immediately after our meal. While we sat around the table and talked about the things of God, Brother Thom pointed a finger at me and said, "Brother, the Lord wants you in full-time ministry and miracles will begin to follow you to confirm this." It just so happened that I was supposed to go to Buckhannon, West Virginia, later that evening to share my testimony at a home prayer meeting.

After a warm farewell, Brother Thom boarded his plane and I left the restaurant to go to my meeting. A friend named Dan Brown was riding with me. On our way to the meeting we came across a young couple whose car had stalled in traffic and was blocking the road. Dan and I got out of our car and asked if we could be of any assistance to them. The young man had the car hood raised and was working on the engine. He informed us that he was a mechanic and there was nothing left to do except push the car out of the way of the traffic and call a tow truck. The engine was flooded and the battery was dead.

Dan and I stood in amazement as the young man began to thoroughly curse his automobile. It was quite offensive to us to hear the name of our Lord used in vain. As I stood there stunned for a moment a verse of scripture came to my mind: *Do not be overcome by evil, but overcome evil with good* (Rom. 12:21). At that moment I felt bold and asked the young man if he would allow me to try to start his car for him.

"I'm a mechanic and I know there is nothing you can do to start this car now," he replied.

"But let me try just one thing," I insisted.

He hesitantly stepped backwards and folded his arms to observe what I was about to do. I leaned over the fender of the car and placed my hand on the air cleaner and prayed aloud: "Heavenly Father, in the name of the Lord Jesus Christ, I ask You to start this man's car right now. Thank You, and amen."

As I raised up I noticed a smirk on the young man's face. I then motioned to the young lady behind the wheel to try to start the car one more time. She did and the car started immediately with no problems. Before I could even say a word to the young man, he slammed the hood down and was running toward the driver's side while the young lady was sliding over to make room for him. He jumped in the car and as he sped past me with a look of bewilderment on his face I heard him mutter, "Ten-Four, Good Buddy." He then took off down the highway with his tires spinning.

Dan and I walked back to our car quite amused at the whole situation. Then I remembered what Brother Thom had said only minutes earlier about miracles following. Dan and I then agreed in prayer asking the Lord to watch over that couple and to save their souls.

I became increasingly more active in the ministry at Christian Communications Center. Joe Rose and I had grown very close in the past months and I often accompanied him on his speaking engagements around the state. The ministry was growing and Joe asked me to consider leaving my job and working with him full time. I didn't feel I was ready for that yet, but Joe kept me busy in all my spare time. He let me host my own television program entitled, "This Little Light." It was patterned after the Christian Broadcasting Network's, "Ross Bagley Show," and was quite successful. I also co-hosted other programs with Joe and felt quite relaxed working on television. Through Joe, I also had the privilege to be the Master of Ceremonies at the "Jesus in '77 Festival" for the Ohio Valley, for which I have continued to serve as M.C. every year since. I was meeting many wonderful people through these opportunites and it appeared that the Lord was beginning to open doors for me.

Some time had passed and Robert Thom was in the Clarksburg area once again to preach. One particular Sunday morning, he was preaching at a church in Fairmont, West Virginia. I arose early that morning to pray before I left my apartment to go to church. I felt sure that the Lord was impressing me to go to the church where Brother Thom was preaching. I didn't immediately obey the voice of the Lord, but instead I went to Sunday School at my own church. All through the Sunday School lesson, I felt uneasy and disobedient. When the lesson was over, I went to Pastor Wilson and shared with him my feelings. He suggested that I go on over to the other church and see Brother Thom. I felt relieved as I drove down the road toward Fairmont.

I walked in the church and found a seat on the front row just as Brother Thom began his message. I hung on to every word that was spoken. At the conclusion of his sermon, Brother Thom asked for the sick and afflicted to come forward and he would pray for them and Jesus would heal them. I was the first one to stand up and go forward for prayer. Although I wasn't sick, I wanted prayer for my eyesight to be corrected. An eye doctor had prescribed reading glasses for me to wear, but I knew the Lord could heal me. As I let my request be made known to Brother Thom, he spoke boldly to me, saying: "Brother, the Lord has something else for you!" Then he turned his back on me and walked to the other side of the church leaving me standing alone. He then lifted his eyes and hands toward heaven and prayed, "Heavenly Father, as You confirmed Your calling on the life of Saul of Tarsus on the road to Damascus, I ask You to now confirm Your calling on this young man's life, in Jesus' name."

Then he turned and looked at me squarely and slowly lowered his arms. At that moment, I felt the Spirit of God come upon me as I never had before. I suddenly felt waves of heat passing through my body and, like a tall tree being chopped down, I fell to the floor with a loud crash and yet I felt no pain. I lay there for several minutes in perfect peace and began to worship the Lord in other tongues as the Holy Spirit gave me utterance. As I continued to lie there on the church floor, the Holy Spirit strongly impressed upon my heart that I would be traveling into Ohio that very day with Brother Thom.

When the service was concluded, I approached Brother Thom, and shyly said, "Brother Thom, I don't want you to think that I'm trying to push myself on you, but I really believe that the Lord has spoken to me to go to Ohio with you today." He just grinned as he opened his hand to me, and on his palm was written in ink the word "Ohio." The Holy Spirit had given Brother Thom a word of knowledge earlier and he had written it on the palm of his hand.

"That's right, Brother," he said, "you're to go to Ohio with me today."

I traveled with Brother Thom into Ohio and watched and listened as he ministered in two separate services. I was able to hear Bible faith taught and then see it put into action. I prayed for the people with Brother Thom after each service and we witnessed the Lord miraculously heal many people and many were filled with the Holy Spirit, with the evidence of speaking in other tongues. Both services reminded me of what I had read that day in Mark 16:20: *And they went out and preached everywhere, while the Lord worked with them, and confirmed the word by the signs that followed.*

When we returned from Ohio, Brother Thom and I had a long talk. "Brother Dan," he said, "I don't believe you will be working in that airplane factory much longer. You have the call of God on your life and you must begin to walk by faith. The Lord will never forsake you. If you should want to be ordained at this time or later, my organization can take care of that for you. I know the Lord has ordained you and that's what is most important."

"Well, Brother Thom," I replied, "give me some time to think it over and pray about it, and also I think I should discuss it with my pastor."

"That's fine, son," he said, "I will keep in touch with you from time to time to see how you're coming along."

The very next day I went to Pastor Wilson and told him about my experience in Ohio and Brother Thom's offer to ordain me. I asked for his advice in the matter. He told me that he would pray about it and discuss it with the elders of the local church, which I had recently joined. An appointment was made for me to talk with the elders and the pastor later that week.

After much discussion we all came to a reasonable agreement. The elders made a promise to me that if I would satisfactorily complete the four years of ministry training offered in the local church that they, through the church, would ordain me and help support my ministry. Since I had become a member of that church and had already completed a year and a half of the required training, I agreed with their decision. I figured that the next couple of years would give me an opportunity to study and learn the Bible more thoroughly and I would be given from time to time the opportunity to minister in the local church.

I thought a lot about what Brother Thom had said about my leaving my job. I didn't want to do something foolish by just quitting my job, so I prayed, "Heavenly Father, I believe You have called me into the ministry and I desire to be obedient to You. If you want me to leave my present job to serve You, I will. But please show me what to do next. In Jesus' name, amen."

20

It was lunch hour at the factory where I worked and I had just sat down to enjoy my sandwich and iced tea. I had picked up a *Voice* magazine to read while I ate my lunch. Many of the employees were reading the *Voice* magazines since I had placed a magazine holder in the main office. It was proving to be an effective witnessing tool there on the job. As I began to read a testimony, two words began to ring over and over again in my head. The words were "hippie" and "happy." I tried to dismiss them and go on reading but the impression would not go away. I went back to work that afternoon with those two words continually rolling around in my head. When I got home from work that evening the words were still following me around. Finally, I prayed, "Heavenly Father, what in the world is going on? What do these two words 'hippie' and 'happy' have to do with me? Are You trying to tell me something?"

Then the Spirit of the Lord began to reveal to me what it all meant. Before I had become a Christian I was always searching for happiness. I tried to do "things" and meet people who would make me happy. But happiness would come and go like the seasons of the year. I thought I would really be happy if I could be a hippie. I let my hair grow long and I quit shaving. I lay around on the beach all day long flirting with the girls and getting high on whatever was available. It was the proverbial "life of Riley" for awhile. Then my hippie happiness faded away like an evening sunset on the beach and I was left with the cold reality of living the everyday drudgery of my life.

Then the Spirit of the Lord began to show me that the pattern of my unhappy life was true in many other people's lives also. I had met people from all walks of life who testified that lasting happiness seemed to elude them. I had met single people who thought marriage would make them happy, but it didn't. I had met married people who thought divorce would make them happy, but it didn't. I thought of how vain their struggles were. I knew business and professional people who thought that success and recognition would make them happy. But their happiness was short lived. Does your life fit into any of these categories?

Suddenly, I realized what was happening. I could see it as clear as a picture. True lasting happiness does not depend on people or circumstances. I had found the answer to my age-old question, "What is life all about?" And the answer had been in the Bible all along. It is found in 1 John 5:11-12: *And the witness is this, that God has given us eternal life, and this is in His Son. He who has the Son has the life; he who does not have the Son of God does not have the life.*

I knew now and had experienced that true and lasting happiness could only be acquired by maintaining an ongoing personal relationship with Jesus Christ, the Son of the living God. I knew that God had worked a real miracle in my life, and I wanted to share that miracle with others in hopes that it would help in leading some unhappy person to a happy life through Jesus Christ.

I asked the Lord to help me write my testimony. After I had completed writing it, I entitled it, "From Hippie to Happy." I knew now what the Lord was up to. He had been encouraging me to write my testimony and mail it to the publishers of *Voice* magazine. I went to my pastor with the idea to get his opinion. He thought it was a good idea but suggested that I remove the title and allow the editors to choose their own title. I willingly agreed. I retyped my testimony without a title and submitted it to the president of our local chapter of the Full Gospel Businessmen's Fellowship International. He agreed to send it in to the publishers of *Voice* magazine for me and assured me that he would inform me whenever he had received word from them.

Several weeks passed by and one day we received a telephone call from California that informed us that the publishers had received my testimony and had decided to publish it. They informed us that it would probably be several months before they published it, however, because they had plenty of advance material to use in their magazine.

The Clarksburg Chapter of the Full Gospel

Businessmen's Fellowship International was presently making preparation for a Good News Telethon that would be produced live at a local television station. The purpose of the telethon was to help spread the "Good News" of Jesus Christ throughout the state of West Virginia. Demos Shakarian, International President and founder of the Full Gospel Businessmen's Fellowship International, and a Good News Telethon Team were coming in from California to produce and direct this telethon in Clarksburg. Many area Christians would be interviewed by Demos concerning how Jesus Christ had changed their lives. I had volunteered my services as a telephone counselor to help handle the incoming telephone calls and requests for prayer.

It just so happened that I arrived at the studio parking lot at the same time as Demos. I had never met Demos before but he warmly greeted me by saying, "Brother, I have something here for you." Then he handed me the July/August 1977 issue of *Voice* magazine which contained my testimony. I turned the pages to where my testimony was and there was the title, "From Hippie to Happy," just as the Lord had shown me months earlier.

It was a surprise and a privilege to be interviewed by Demos Shakarian on the Good News Telethon. I simply shared with the viewers how the Lord Jesus Christ had brought happiness into my life and could do the same for them. Afterwards, Demos and I had the opportunity to talk and pray together. Demos said that he believed the Lord was going to use my life for His glory and he prayed with me that the Lord would send me around the world with the Good News.

In August 1977, after a very successful Good News Telethon, it was time for the Full Gospel Businessmen's Regional Convention to be held in West Virginia. A three-day convention was scheduled for Thursday, Friday and Saturday, August 18, 19, and 20, 1977, at the Sheraton Inn in Clarksburg. There were many wonderful speakers and teachers on hand to instruct us in the Word of God. There was a real spirit of expectancy in the air.

On Saturday afternoon I was asked to drive Charles

Capps, one of the convention speakers, to the local airport and pick up Tom Ashcraft, who was scheduled to speak at the Saturday evening meeting. Upon returning to the lobby of the Sheraton Inn, I noticed several young men dressed in tuxedos and several young ladies dressed alike in long, flowing gowns. As I looked over the group, I noticed that one young lady was Nina's sister, Cindy. I walked across the lobby to greet her. After conversing with Cindy for a few minutes, I learned that this was Nina's wedding day and that the wedding party had followed the bride and groom to the hotel. For a moment I was stunned and didn't know what to think or say. Just as I felt I had regained my composure, I turned around and stood face to face with Nina.

Our eyes met for only a few fleeting seconds but they seemed to capture eternity. My mind quickly recounted all of our past times together. I hadn't seen Nina for well over a year and I thought that my feelings for her had gone. But at that moment I knew deep inside of me that I really hadn't forgotten her and I wondered why this unscheduled rendezvous had to happen. As I began to drift back into the reality of the situation that confronted me, I sincerely congratulated her and her husband, Max, and wished them the best in everything. As they walked away together, I suddenly felt a release from deep within me, and I prayed that they really would have a successful and lasting marriage.

I walked outside to the parking lot and watched them drive away. Then I asked the Lord why this whole episode had taken place. A verse of scripture quickly came to mind, Romans 8:28: *And we know that God causes all things to work together for good to those who love God, to those who are called according to His purpose.*

I began to understand more clearly what the Lord was showing me. When Nina had broken up with me, I felt that it was the worst tragedy that had ever befallen me in my life. In those dark, depressing times, I cried out to God for help and He heard me. He turned my tragedy into something good, for through the loss of Nina, I found a true and lasting happiness with Jesus Christ. I knew at that moment that all my old bridges were burnt behind me and I had an exciting future ahead of me. I knew that this rendezvous with Nina was not an accident or a coincidence. It was the Lord's way of telling me to forget the past and to press on to the things ahead. That is just what I did.

Robert Thom's words to me had come to pass. The airplane factory where I had worked for the past three years laid me off. I was now without a job and had plenty of time on my hands to do whatever the Lord gave me to do. As a result of my testimony appearing in *Voice* magazine, I was invited to speak at Full Gospel Businessmen's chapters all around the state of West Virginia and in several surrounding states. Brother Joe Rose kept me busy doing television programs at Christian Communications Center. I began to receive invitations from various churches to come and preach and share my testimony. I was also spending much time at my home church, learning about ministry in the local church.

On March 13, 1978, the church hired me to be the pastor's secretary and help him with the work in the church office. The church was steadily growing and prospering and had decided to open a Christian school for grades K through twelve in the fall of that year. I was also hired to be the secretary of the Christian school. Between television programs and speaking engagements, plus working at the church and school, the Lord was really keeping me busy. And I was truly enjoying every minute of it. I constantly prayed that the Lord would use me in greater capacities.

As time went by, I recognized within my heart a growing desire to travel around the world with the Gospel message of our Lord Jesus Christ.

21

As I travel from place to place, more and more I meet people who have received lasting happiness through a personal relationship with Jesus Christ. But to be perfectly honest, I also see the other side of the coin. I meet many unhappy people, including Christians, wherever I go. I can understand why a person who isn't a Christian would be unhappy. I also know that if a Christian doesn't maintain a close relationship with Jesus Christ, he can also lose his happiness. Jesus said that if *we* allowed the cares of this world, the deceitfulness of riches and the lust for other things to enter into our lives, then His words would be choked out of us and we would become unhappy again. But it doesn't have to be that way for you!

A preacher once said to me, "Dan, when everything around you seems to be getting too tough to handle, don't ever run from God, always run to God." I've always remembered that and practiced it, and it really works for me. It will work for you too. Don't ever give up! I've had a lot of disappointments and I've been hurt by many people, especially well-meaning Christians, since I've become a Christian. But I can truthfully say that Jesus Christ has never once hurt me or disappointed me in anything. I have learned valuable lessons from my disappointments and hurts. One of those lessons is "always keep your eyes on Jesus." He is the author and the finisher of our faith, not people. When we place our faith and trust in people and organizations, instead of in the Lord, we are in danger of great disappointment. But if we consistently place our faith and trust in Jesus, then He can use people and organizations to bless our lives. Allow me to share with you some of my experiences.

The year 1978 proved to be a busy and productive year for me, as well as a happy one. I entered 1979 expecting more of the same. But some things took place during 1979 that really rocked my boat and caused me to begin to wonder if everything was worth it.

I was busy working at the local church and Christian school, plus traveling on weekends and evenings to speak at various meetings. Joe Rose and I were also busy doing television programs and frequently traveling together to speak to different groups of people about our faith in Jesus Christ. Joe was constantly encouraging me to come and work with him on a full-time basis. We had made some plans to do several things together during that year. But our plans were never realized. On April 18, 1979, Joe's life on earth was suddenly cut short and he got to go to heaven a lot sooner than anybody had expected. It was a shock to the entire Christian community. Joe and I had been scheduled to speak together at some meetings and I had to make telephone calls and explain why we wouldn't be there.

The event of Joe's untimely death seemed to be the beginning of many disappointments and changes in my life. Christian Communication Center was now under new leadership, and shortly after Joe's promotion to heaven, I received a letter from the new management stating that "under the circumstances" my services would no longer be required at the center. The problem with that was that nobody ever took the time to explain to me what the circumstances were that we were under. I was a little hurt at first, but after I prayed about the situation it seemed that the Lord was encouraging me all the more to trust Him totally and that He would work everything out for my good. I also remembered some good advice that a minister had once given me. He said, "Dan, God never allows a door to be closed in your face without opening a greater door of opportunity elsewhere." That advice was a real comfort to me then.

I was no longer involved in television ministry, so I figured that I would have more time to devote to traveling and speaking at various meetings. Besides, I was scheduled to be ordained by the local church on July 1, 1979, and to launch out into full-time evangelistic ministry. My four years of training were now completed and the elders of the local church were about to fulfill their agreement with me by ordaining me and helping me to get established in the ministry. I was really anxious to get started.

Then another disappointment occurred. The elders of the local church had become displeased with the pastor over some controversial issues. They called together an official board meeting and the result of that meeting was that on June 16, 1979, the pastor was dismissed from his position as leader of the church. The congregation continued for many months without a pastor. This caused a lot of confusion and unrest among the people. Because I had been the pastor's secretary, I soon found myself without a position. School had been dismissed for the summer months, therefore my work as the secretary of the Christian school was also eliminated.

I became concerned about my ordination, so I requested an audience with the board of elders in order to discuss the situation. The result of the discussion was that the elders felt that they could not fulfill their promise to ordain me on July 1, as we had previously agreed. Perhaps at some later date it would be possible, but no promises could be made. My only thought was, "Well, Lord, what else could possibly happen to make me unhappy?"

The answer came soon enough. On July 13 my faithful automobile, which had logged well over one hundred thousand miles, simply refused to run. After a thorough inspection by a local mechanic, the verdict was that I would have to invest a small fortune in that car if it were ever to run again. Then to make things even more frustrating, suddenly I was receiving no invitations to preach or speak at any meetings. It just seemed that nobody was interested in hearing what I had to say at that time. I felt that I had finally come to the end of my proverbial rope and was hanging on by a mere thread. In my desperation I cried out as Jesus had on the cross, "My God, my God, why have You forsaken me?"

In the period of a few short months, it seemed that everything had happened to steal the happiness I had once known from serving the Lord. I had lost the television programs, I had lost my positions as the church and Christian school secretary, I had no invitations to speak anywhere, no money, no car, no income and no explanation for any of it.

The people who were once my close friends and even brothers and sisters in the family of God appeared to want little or nothing to do with me. I still loved the Lord. I had not committed any sin. "Why, why, why?" I questioned. I prayed, and prayed, and prayed for the answers to come. But it seemed that the only answer I received from God was silence. I thought I heard a still small voice from deep within me saying, "Don't worry about a thing, My son, everything will work out fine for you." But by this time, it was difficult for me to really believe that God still cared about me, and was speaking to me. I felt forsaken by everybody!

I was scheduled to be the Master of Ceremonies for the "Jesus in '79 Festival" in Vincent, Ohio, on August 2, 3, and 4, 1979. This was my third year in a row as the M.C. of the festival and I was really looking forward to just getting away from Clarksburg and enjoying the fellowship of other Christians at the festival. I had to borrow a car in order to get there. Robert Thom was one of the scheduled speakers and I was looking forward to seeing him again. It had been several months since I had last talked with him and he knew nothing of what I had been going through.

On Saturday, August 3, I saw Brother Thom walking across the camp grounds in my direction. When he saw me, the first words out of his mouth were, "Brother, I told you that that church would never ordain you. Now you must get busy and do the Lord's work. Time is running out, you know!"

I was amazed. Later, Brother Thom told me that the Lord had shown him what had been happening to me. Before we parted company, he took me by the hand and prayed, "Heavenly Father, may Thy precious anointing rest upon my brother and bless all the works of his hands. In Jesus' name, it shall be done, amen."

And then he began to prophesy: "Thus saith the Lord God, I, even I, the Lord Almighty shall bless and keep thee and thou shalt travel into many countries and preach the Gospel to them in their native tongue, even though you have never learned their tongue, and I will be with thee and strengthen thee and keep thee in all thy ways, saith the Lord."

When Brother Thom left that day, he promised to keep in touch with me. His last words to me were, "Keep that smile on your face for Jesus, Brother!" I returned to Clarksburg somewhat encouraged and wondering what the Lord was about to do next in my life.

Pastor Wilson had taken a step of faith and started a new church in the Clarksburg area. I decided to attend some of the services and I talked with him about what was happening in my life. He simply encouraged me to trust Jesus and everything would work out for the best. The people in the congregation were very kind and showed a genuine concern about my future in the ministry. On August 22, 1979, one of the members of that congregation gave me an automobile. It was a used Buick Electra that was in excellent condition. To me, this was a miracle from God. My prayer had been answered and my faith was strengthened. I continually praised the Lord for that car. It was time for me to take Brother Thom's advice to heart and totally walk by faith.

I felt led by the Holy Spirit to begin a Bible study and prayer meeting in the town of Buckhannon, West Virginia, which is about twenty-five miles south of Clarksburg. The Bible study began on Tuesday evening, September 18, 1979, with about seven people. The people asked me to come back on Sunday morning and teach them. After that, we decided to meet twice weekly to systematically study the truths in God's Word. A few invitations began to come to me to preach in various area churches, and I gratefully accepted every one. This is the way the Lord provided for my financial needs, through the love offerings and honorariums that I received at these various meetings.

While I was preparing to go to church one Sunday morning, I turned the television set on to watch the Ernest Angley Hour. Reverend Angley was announcing that he was taking a tour of the Holy Land. The tour would leave New York City on December 31, 1979, and return on January 11, 1980. The entire cost of the tour was $1,295.00. which included all the expenses while visiting the countries of Egypt, Jordan and Israel. Even as a little Sunday

School boy I remembered thinking what a wonderful experience it would be to visit the land where Jesus was born and lived. Since I had become a born-again Christian, I had a deep desire to visit the nation of Israel. But it seemed like an utter impossibility for me to even think of such a trip. I had no money and no income that would allow for such an expensive trip. And yet as Reverend Angley spoke, I could almost see myself there walking in the footsteps of Jesus. That morning I knelt in prayer and asked my Heavenly Father in Jesus' name to make this impossibility a reality for me. Jesus once said in Matthew 21:22: *"And all things you ask in prayer, believing, you shall receive."*

The next day I mailed a letter to Reverend Angley and requested more information about the trip. In a few days I received a reply that stated I would have to send a $200.00 deposit in order to reserve a seat on the airplane. I didn't have $200.00 so I desperately prayed for some direction. After praying, I went to my dad and asked him if I could borrow $200.00 and told him what I planned to do with it.

"Well, son," he said, "I'll be happy to give you the first $200.00 for that trip, but God will have to supply you the rest."

"Thanks, Dad," I replied, "And I believe that somehow the Lord will supply the rest."

My faith was lifted as I mailed in the deposit money. I just simply believed that I was on my way. Over the period of the next several months I began to tell people that I was going to Israel, and daily I thanked the Lord in my prayers for supplying the needed money.

Little by little I began to receive donations from different people who said they wanted to help me out on my trip. My heart was deeply touched by their thoughtfulness and generosity. The deadline date to have my money paid in full was November 15, 1979. On November 14, 1979, by God's grace, I had been able to save $845.00, but that was still $250.00 short of my final goal. That night, with checkbook in hand, I knelt and prayed, "Dear Heavenly Father, I believe in my heart that it is Your will for me to make this pilgrimage to Israel. My money must be paid by tomorrow and I am lacking $250.00 of the full amount. I am going to write a check now for the full amount of $1,095.00 and I am asking You in the name of my Lord Jesus Christ to work a miracle for me and provide the $250.00 that I don't have at this time. Thank You for supplying my every need, amen."

The next morning I went to the post office to mail my check. That same moring I received a check for $350.00 from a dear Christian lady who was 101 years old. She simply said, "Danny, I want to make sure that you get to visit the Holy Land." I praised the Lord with great expectations as I hurried to the bank to deposit the $350.00 check. Then I wrote a check for $100.00 and gave it to somebody more needy than me, because I've learned that the words of the Lord are true, " *It is more blessed to give than to receive*" (Acts 20:35).

On December 31, 1979, New Year's Eve, I found myself seated in a 747 Jumbo Jet airliner, some 40,000 feet above the Atlantic Ocean, on my to Israel and singing along as Reverend Angley led us all in a chorus of "Only believe, only believe, all things are possible, only believe."

When we landed in Amman, Jordan, I learned that my assigned roommate had had to cancel his trip at the last minute and my new roommate was a businessman from St. Louis, Missouri, whose name was Peter. Peter was a friend of Reverend Angley and also a friend of Mr. Campbell, the man who owned Christian Fellowship Tours. Mr. Campbell had arranged our tour so that it was first class all the way. Peter and I became great friends from the very beginning and we were able to share many wonderful experiences together in the Holy Land.

Our first stop was in Cairo, Egypt, where we were able to stay at the Mena House Hotel, the oldest and nicest hotel in Egypt. The pyramids were just a walk across the street from our hotel. It was exciting as we rode our camels across the sands to visit the great pyramid of King Cheop. We visited the land of Goshen where the children of Israel were protected from the wrath of God, as the ten plagues were poured out upon Pharaoh and the Egyptians.

This was the land where Moses had once lived. I stood

face to face before the aging Sphinx and wondered at the many sunrises that must have shone upon his decaying face. We toured the Egyptian museum and viewed the many treasures of King Tut. But my heart began to rise with an indescribable feeling as we crossed the Jordanian border and entered the land of Israel.

This was my first visit to Israel and yet I felt as if I were returning home. We visited the Dead Sea and Qumran, where the Dead Sea Scrolls were discovered by a shepherd in 1947. We passed through Jericho and viewed the Mount of Temptation and stopped for a refreshing drink of sweet water at Elisha's fountain. We went for a boat ride on the beautiful Sea of Galilee and toured the town of Capernaum, where Jesus had performed so many mighty miracles.

Reverend Angley held a water baptismal service in the Jordan River, and then we were on our way to "The Holy City," Jerusalem. We stopped in the town of Caesarea Philippi, where Jesus asked the question of His disciples, *"Who do people say that I am?"* (Mark 8:27). And then on to a magnificent view from atop Mount Carmel, the spot where Elijah the prophet had called down fire from heaven.

We passed through the plains of Megiddo, where the Battle of Armageddon will one day be fought, and together we sang hymns as we entered the town of Nazareth, the boyhood home of Jesus. The last few days of our trip were spent in Jerusalem, where we stayed in the luxurious Intercontinental Hotel nestled comfortably atop the Mount of Olives.

The city of Jerusalem is filled with a wealth of historic sites, and we spent several days just roaming the city and surrounding area. We visited the Church of the Nativity, in Bethlehem, built upon the spot where once a stable stood and where our Lord Jesus was born nearly two thousand years ago. I knelt down in the tomb of Lazarus and read the account of his death and resurrection from John's Gospel, chapter eleven. We toured the inside of the Dome of the Rock, and later I washed my hands and feet in the Pool of Bethesda. Later we walked the Via Dolorosa and

Reverend Angley held a "Holy Ghost Rally" in the Upper Room, the traditional spot where the Holy Spirit first came upon the early disciples of Jesus on the day of Pentecost, and the Christian Church was born. We prayed at the Western Wall (Wailing Wall) and, later that evening, we stood upon the Mount of Ascension, the spot where Jesus will one day soon set His foot down upon this earth again.

But my two most unforgettable experiences took place in the Garden of Gethsemane at the Rock of Agony, and then at the Garden Tomb, the place where our Lord Jesus Christ was resurrected from the dead.

I was kneeling in prayer at the Rock of Agony, in the Garden of Gethsemane. This is the spot believed to be spoken of in Luke 22:39-44 where Jesus agonized in prayer to the point that *his sweat was as it were great drops of blood falling down to the ground* (v. 44 KJV). I was earnestly praying for unity in the many churches and asking the Lord to somehow use me in His ministry. I lifted up my hands toward heaven in praise to God, when suddenly I felt something unusual happening. It felt as if someone were pouring warm honey down over my hands and arms. Then suddenly the Spirit of the Lord spoke to my heart in a voice that literally melted me, saying, "Take My healing power to all nations!"

The next day, Reverend Angley was conducting a communion service at the Garden Tomb. I was inside the tomb, kneeling in prayer, when once again the Spirit of the Lord came upon me as He had at the Rock of Agony, and this time He said, "Take My resurrection power to all nations!"

During the remainder of my stay in Israel, I found my mind occupied with thoughts of these two occurrences. My mind was flooded with so many questions. "How will I go to all nations? Where will the money come from? Where do I go first?" My mind seemed like a raging storm, while my heart was experiencing calm peace. It seemed that the Lord was saying, "I will provide for you all things at the appointed time and you will know that it is I, the Lord, who does all things well."

On the last day of our trip, I talked with Reverend

Angley about my experiences and asked him for his advice and his prayers for me. His advice to me was: "Pray and fast often, and study God's Word. He will guide you by His Spirit." I've earnestly tried to follow that advice.

On our plane ride back to the United States I was reading Jimmy Swaggart's monthly magazine, *The Evangelist*. Jimmy Swaggart was advertising a trip to South Africa from March 8, 1980, through March 25, 1980, for a total cost of $2,795.00. I was showing the article to Peter when he said, "Mr. Campbell's tour agency is handling that tour to South Africa for Jimmy Swaggart." Then he added, "You should consider going on that trip. I think it would be good for you to meet Jimmy Swaggart and get to know him."

I answered, "Well, Peter, I'd love to go to South Africa and I'd love to meet Jimmy Swaggart, but the cost of the trip is $2,795.00 and my only income is from love offerings and honorariums that I receive. If the Lord wants me to go to South Africe and meet Jimmy Swaggart, then He will have to perform quite a financial miracle for me." That was the end of our conversation concerning the South African trip.

We arrived back in New York City on Friday, January 11, 1980. Peter and I promised to stay in touch as we departed to catch our planes home. I arrived safely and was excited to tell my parents and friends about the wonderful experiences that I'd had in Israel. But soon I was saddened by the news that Robert Thom had been promoted to heaven on Saturday, January 12, 1980. I was happy for him, but sad because I would dearly miss him. He had said on many occasions that he would like for me to travel to South Africa, and told me of the years he had spent living in the Methodist orphanage a few miles outside the city of Cape Town after his father had died. South Africa seemed so far, far away.

22

On Saturday, February 16, 1980, I received a nice letter from Peter and enclosed was a check for $3,000.00. The Lord had directed Peter to send me to South Africa with Jimmy Swaggart. To me, this was a tremendous miracle.

On Saturday, March 8, 1980, at about 4:30 p.m., I was introduced to Jimmy Swaggart in the lobby of the J.F.K. International Airport in New York. There were about thirty people scheduled to make this journey to South Africa and approximately eighteen of those were Jimmy Swaggart's crusade team members. We all sat around the airport lobby and got acquainted, while waiting for our plane. We also enjoyed some of my mother's homemade banana nut bread, while Jimmy sat and read my testimony "From Hippie to Happy," from a copy of *Voice* magazine I had given him.

We arrived in Johannesburg, South Africa, on Sunday, March 9, 1980, around 5:45 p.m. As we stepped off the airplane, Jimmy's little granddaughter, Jennifer, looked around the airport and then looked up at Jimmy and said, "Paw-Paw, where is da elfanants at?"

I immediately noticed a man wearing a Full Gospel Businessmen's Fellowship lapel pin and I introduced myself to him.

"Hi, I'm Dan Nicholson and I noticed your lapel pin," I said. "I'm also a member of the Full Gospel Businessmen's Fellowship."

"Pleased to meet you, Brother Nicholson," he replied. "My name is Harold Horn." Then Harold asked me, "What is your occupation, Brother?"

"Well, I'm an evangelist and I came on this journey under the direction of the Holy Spirit," I answered.

"Well, praise the Lord," said Harold. "We'll have to get you some meetings while you're in South Africa."

"Amen to that," I agreed.

A few minutes later I met Peter and Mr. Campbell in the airport lobby. It was really great to see both of them again. They had arrived in South Africa a few days ahead of us in order to get all the details in order for our arrival and stay there. We spent just a little time in the airport before catching another flight which took us to the city of Durban. Upon our arrival in Durban, we were lodged in the beautiful Royal Hotel for the next four days. Jimmy Swaggart was scheduled to hold a city-wide crusade in Durban.

On Monday morning, Mr. Campbell, Peter and I toured the City of Durban, and in the afternoon we caught a taxi cab and drove to "The Valley of a Thousand Hills" to visit a Zulu tribal village. It was a very exciting and educational visit. On Tuesday, Mr. Campbell, Peter, and I took a boat tour on the Indian Ocean, and that evening we attended the Jimmy Swaggart Crusade at the Sugar Bowl in Durban. There were thousands of blacks, whites and coloreds (mulattoes) in attendance that night and the Lord blessed the meeting tremendously. Then, Wednesday morning, around 6:00 a.m., Mr. Campbell and Peter caught a plane to return to the United States.

Those of us who remained in South Africa arrived in Kruger National Park on Friday afternoon and at 6:30 p.m. we enjoyed a meal of barbecued Impala (a kind of deer) together. It was exciting to see all the big game animals running free in their natural habitat.

We arrived back in Johannesburg around 5:00 p.m. on Saturday, March 15, 1980, where we were lodged in the Rosebank Hotel. During the day we toured the city and visited many historical sites, including the Simmer and Jack Gold Mine. In the evenings we attended the Jimmy Swaggart Crusade, which proved to be tremendously successful. On Wednesday morning, at 6:30 a.m., the crusade team flew on to Cape Town, but I stayed behind in Johannesburg an extra day, because I had been given the opportunity to preach the Gospel on foreign soil and it was an exciting experience for me. The Lord blessed the occasion and many people were baptized in the Holy Spirit and healed of various diseases in that meeting.

I arrived in Cape Town around 1:00 p.m. Thursday afternoon and joined the rest of our group at the Newlands Hotel. Upon my arrival I was notified that I would have the opportunity to preach in two different churches on

Sunday, March 23, 1980. I eagerly awaited the privilege.

I caught a train into the city of Cape Town on Friday and just spent the day walking around and viewing the sights. Later in the day I took a taxi cab to the cable car station that would lift me over 3,700 feet to the top of Table Mountain.

Cape Town, South Africa, is one of the most beautiful cities in the world, but you haven't seen the city until you've seen it from the top of Table Mountain. The view is breathtakingly beautiful and beyond my ability to describe. I was so taken with the view that I returned on Saturday and spent the entire day just walking around on top of the mountain. While on the mountain I spent much time in prayer seeking the direction of the Lord concerning the two services I would have the privilege to preach on Sunday. I ate a delicious steak dinner at the mountain top restaurant and sat back comfortably to watch the magnificent sunset on the Indian Ocean.

That night I returned to my room in the Newlands Hotel and went to bed early. Sometime in the early hours I had an unusual dream. In that dream I saw myself preaching in a small church. At the conclusion of my sermon I asked for people to come forward who desired prayer for various reasons. The first person who came for prayer was a lady who was blind in one eye. In the dream I saw myself praying for the lady and instantly the Lord restored her vision. Then from off to my right side there came a deaf man requesting prayer that he might hear. Immediately after I prayed for him the Lord restored the man's hearing. Then the Holy Spirit began to sweep over that congregation and many miraculous healings took place. With that, the dream ended.

I arose at 6:00 a.m. on Sunday morning, March 23, 1980. After the normal morning preparations, I went outside for a walk. The air was fresh and crisp and I ambled along the sidewalk outside the hotel. I began to think upon the sovereignty of God. The Lord had sent a man named Robert Thom from Cape Town, South Africa, to a small town in the hills of West Virginia. This man had laid his hands upon my head and prophesied that God would use me to perform miracles in the lives of other people. Now Robert Thom was in heaven and here I stood in Cape Town, where he had come from. My thoughts were interrupted by a voice, "Are you Reverend Nicholson?"

"Yes, may I help you?" I replied.

"I'm the pastor of the church where you will be preaching this morning and we really must be going," he said.

The little church was filled with people and the Lord gave me an inspiring message to deliver. When I had concluded my sermon, I asked for people to come forward who desired prayer for various reasons. The first person in line for prayer was a lady who was somewhat crippled with arthritis and blind in one eye. I prayed for God to heal her and immediately her crippled joints were loosed from the arthritis. She was also able to see perfectly through her eye that moments earlier had been completely blind. She began to shout, "Glory to God, glory to God," and to dance down the church aisle.

I immediately thought of the dream I'd had the night before. I looked off to my right side and sure enough there stood a man who was deaf and requesting prayer that God would restore his hearing. Immediately after we prayed, the man could hear perfectly with the ears that were once dead to sound. The Holy Spirit then began to sweep over that congregation and the people were responding. Nineteen people received the baptism in the Holy Spirit while seven people came forward and received Jesus Christ as their personal Savior. Many others were healed of various ailments. My dream had become a reality right before my eyes. In the evening service I preached at a different church and witnessed more of the same results. People were born again, healed, and baptized in the Holy Spirit with the evidence of speaking in other tongues.

I arose early on Monday morning to pray and take another walk before catching a bus that would take us to the airport at 12:30 p.m. Our plane was scheduled to leave for Rome, Italy, at 4:00 p.m. As I walked around the hotel parking lot pondering what had happened in the church services the day before, it was then that I really realized that God actually was working all things together for my good. For a short time I thought God had forsaken me, but I could see now that it was only that He had greater plans for me than I had for myself. I looked up toward heaven with tears in my eyes and said, "Heavenly Father, forgive me for ever doubting Your love for me. Thank You for taking care of me and using me in Your ministry. And also Lord, please let Brother Thom see what You're doing down here with me. In Jesus' name, amen."

We arrived in Rome, Italy, around noon on Monday, March 24, 1980. We had a nice lunch in a little cafe and spent the remainder of the day touring the city. I stood silently for a few minutes in the prison where tradition says the Apostle Paul had been held prisoner before his execution. Under the inspiration of the Holy Spirit, he had written most of the New Testament. I tried to imagine what it must have been like for him at the time he was imprisoned in that dungeon hole. Then I remembered what he had written in his letter to the Philippians in chapter four, verse thirteen: *I can do all things through Him who strengthens me.* Even in the face of death, we need not fear for Jesus will give us strength to see us through.

We toured the Vatican, St. Peter's Basilica and finally the Roman Coliseum. Jimmy Swaggart and I walked around the Coliseum together and discussed the fact that many Christians had been brutally murdered on those grounds and that many were even fed to the lions because they refused to deny their faith in the Lordship of Jesus Christ. We both agreed that someday soon we will meet those saints face to face and rejoice together through all eternity with our Lord Jesus Christ.

I awoke at 7:00 a.m., Friday morning, March 28, 1980, safe and secure in my little apartment in Clarksburg, West Virginia. I lay there comfortably and stared at the ceiling, while mentally I was reviewing my life. "Could all of these things really be true?" I questioned. And yet I knew that they were because they had happened to me.

I really have found the happiness that I so longed for in my life. It comes from having a personal relationship with my Lord Jesus Christ. Now I know I have a purpose for living. As I lay quietly upon my bed, I couldn't help wondering what adventure the Lord had in store for me next.

As the month of April 1980, was coming to a close, a friend asked me if I would like to accompany him to Washington, D.C., to attend a rally called "Washington For Jesus." It was a gathering of born-again Christians from every state in the union and from some other countries. The purpose of the rally was to gather together in our nation's capital and pray for our country and for those government officials whose responsibility it is to govern the nation. Many Christians believe that our country needs to repent of her sins and cry out to God for His mercy. The theme of the rally was 2 Chronicles 7:14: *If my people, which are called by my name, shall humble themselves, and pray, and seek my face, and turn from their wicked ways; then will I hear from heaven, and will forgive their sin, and will heal their land* (KJV).

The rally proved to be perhaps the largest Christian gathering in the history of the United States. There were hundreds of thousands of people in attendance who came to simply ask for God's forgiveness and to pray for a revival in our land of true faith in the living God. There were many wonderful speakers addressing the crowds while we were there. One speaker stood out to me among all the others. He was the Reverend John Giminez. As I listened intently to him encourage the people to pray, my mind rushed back to the first time I had heard him preach. It had been his personal testimony that had inspired me to believe on the Lord Jesus Christ. How happy I am now that I took John's advice. As I continued to listen to him speak, I silently prayed, "Dear Lord Jesus, please continue to bless and use John Giminez for Your glory."

After returning home from Washington, I was busy preaching at various meetings when in July the opportunity came for me to spend a couple of weeks in California. While in California I made some wonderful new friends and had the opportunity to see how really beautiful that part of the country is. I toured San Diego, Los Angeles, Hollywood, San Francisco and then traveled on up the coast into Oregon and Washington. My main observation was that people are basically the same wherever you go. We all face the same problems and questions of life. How happy I am to tell people wherever I go that regardless of what their problems may be, Jesus Christ is ultimately their answer.

In December, I received an unexpected telephone call from my friend Peter, who had been my roommate in Israel and had sent me to South Africa with Jimmy Swaggart.

"Dan, do you have a busy schedule in January, 1981?" he questioned.

"No, Peter, I've actually got nothing scheduled for January, as of now," I replied. "Why do you ask?"

"Well," he said, "how would you like to go to China?"

"China!" I said, "You mean THE China?"

"Yes Dan, our friend Wayne is taking a small group of Christians into China in January and I'd like for you to go along. Can you?"

"I'd love to go Peter," I replied.

"Good," he said, "I'll call you back in a few days with all the details." Then we said goodbye.

Three days later Peter called again and said, "Dan, your tickets are in the mail and I'll meet you at Los Angeles International Airport on January 4, 1981."

We concluded our conversation and I hung up my telephone. I sat down in a chair and began to think: "This is absolutely miraculous. The Lord by His grace is giving me my heart's desire to travel around the world and I have very little to do with it." I sat and fought back tears. Only the Lord knew how much these travels mean to me, and because of His love for me, He is allowing me to have what I asked Him for. Then I remembered the words of Jesus recorded in Mark 9:23: *If thou canst believe, all things are possible to him that believeth (KJV).* I also thought of the words of the great Apostle Paul found in Romans 8:32: *He that spared not his own Son, but delivered him up for us all, how shall he not with him also freely give us all things? (KJV).*

Then I began to realize that God really does love us

all, that He gave the life of His Son Jesus for us all, and that through Jesus He also freely gives us all things. Not many preachers preach that kind of a message, and yet it is the Word of God. Jesus Christ was not tempting us or teasing us when He said in John 15:7: *If ye abide in me, and my words abide in you, ye shall ask what ye will, and it shall be done unto you* (*KJV*). He meant what He said and He's saying it to you!

January 4 came quickly and I was excited to meet Peter at the L.A. International Airport. We spent the night with some dear friends in Los Angeles and the next day we left for our adventure in China. There were twelve of us on this trip and we met and got acquainted in the airport lobby. I was happy to find out the Reverend Jim Rentz would be traveling with us. Jim is a member of the Jimmy Swaggart organization and was my roommate while I was traveling in South Africa. We all laughed when someone compared us to God's twelve spies spoken of in Numbers, chapter 13. Now we really felt like we were commissioned by God to go and spy out the land of China. We were all very excited.

Our first stop was in Seoul, Korea, where we all enjoyed a Korean style lunch and a bus tour of the city. Our tour included a visit to the Full Gospel Church, acclaimed to be the largest church in the world. When we were there, we were told that the membership was in excess of 150,000 people. The pastor is the Reverend Paul Yonggi Cho. Pastor Cho is certainly experiencing the blessing of the Lord upon his congregation.

Our next stop was only to refuel the plane in Japan's second largest city, Osaka, and then on to Tiapai, Taiwan, where we had a layover of several hours. We were allowed the opportunity to do a little shopping and looking around. Then we went on to Hong Kong where we spent three days as guests of the beautiful New World Hotel. Our stay there was marvelous. We enjoyed wonderful meals and professionally conducted city tours. There was an exciting ferry ride across the famous Hong Kong Harbor and lunch at the Jumbo Seafood Restaurant, the largest floating seafood restaurant in the world. The excitement mounted as we prepared for a two-week journey into the mainland of China. We made contact with some Assemblies of God missionaries in Hong Kong and were able to secure an ample supply of Gospel tracts printed in Chinese. We really did feel like God's smugglers as we crossed the border into China by train.

The first stop in mainland China was the city of Canton. We were amazed at some of the sites in Canton. One of the buildings we toured was over six hundred years old. "This building is three times older than your country," our guide proudly proclaimed. Our guide was very well educated and gave us some interesting statistics. He informed us that in China there are 55 national minorities which total about 55.8 million people, or about 6% of China's total population, which now exceeds 1 billion people. The average wage in China is about 60 yen per month, an equivalent of $40.00.

Communal living is very popular in China and we had the opportunity to visit a commune and observe how they raise their own food and share their living quarters. The Chinese appeared to be very kind and loving people with very high moral standards. Our guide said that in order to be married in China, the man should be 25 years old and the lady should be 23 years old. The Chinese believe that a young couple should have their educations completed and be mature before assuming the responsibilities of marriage. Oftentimes after marriage the bride will simply move in with the groom in his parents' home. The family is a very respected establishment in China and because of over-population at this time the government is strongly recommending and rewarding families for birth control.

I was overwhelmed by the crowds of people and the thousands of bicycles I saw in China. Our guide told us that there are over 300 million bicycles in China, which amounts to approximately one bicycle for every three people. The bicycles cost about $100.00 a piece, which is about two and one half months' wages. Therefore, the bicycles are usually bought on time. It takes the average Chinese more than a year to pay for a bicycle.

Our next stop was the enchanting city of Shanghai.

There we visited the world-famous waterfront and subtly distributed Gospel tracts. The people seemed so very hungry for us to communicate with them. We also attended a church service in Shanghai. It was called the Community Church and there was standing room only. The Christians there told us that the church had only been open for about three weeks. One lady, who could speak English very well, told us that this was the first time in over thirty years as a Christian that she was permitted to attend a public worship service. It does appear that God has opened a door for the Gospel message to be proclaimed in China. But only He knows how long that door will remain open. We must earnestly pray that God will use our Christian brothers and sisters in China to reach the millions of lost souls there before it is too late.

From Shanghai we traveled to Nanjing. The Yangste River, which is the third largest river in the world, flows through the city. We had the privilege of enjoying a wonderful boat ride on the Yangste River in what was at one time Mao-Tse-Tung's private boat. We visited the Sun Yat Sen Mausoleum and later were taken to an evening at the theater. The Chinese are very talented entertainers. During these tours, we all remained in constant prayer that God would give us opportunities to be His ambassadors. And we took advantage of every opportunity. Our guides were anxious to listen as we shared with them our faith in Jesus Christ. As we would travel from stop to stop and have to change guides, our former guides were always saddened to see us go. They loved to hear us sing, Oddly enough though, the song most requested by the Chinese was, "Jingle Bells." We were constantly singing our favorite Christian choruses as we traveled across China and we could see that the Holy Spirit was reaching out to touch their hearts with God's love. We usually parted from our guides with tears and hugs.

Our last stop going north was the beautiful city of Bejing, or more often called Peking. We had the privilege of touring the majestic Forbidden City, where the famed dynasties of China once lived and ruled. We also visited the Ming Tombs, the Summer Palace, the Temple of

Heaven and finally the incredible Great Wall of China. We were told that one of our astronauts commented that the Great Wall of China is the only man-made object on earth that can be clearly seen from outer space. Students from the Peking University gave us a wonderfully skillful performance of the ballet, "Swan Lake," one evening.

Our last evening in Peking was celebrated with a scrumptious Peking Duck dinner, along with a Mongolian Hot Pot. What a treat! We were soon on the train again and crossing the border back into Hong Kong. Overall, we believed the entire journey was a real success. We had a first-hand view of China's mainland and a real opportunity to appraise the needs of the people there. I believe that all Christians should remember to pray for the salvation of the Chinese people and to do whatever we can to see that Bibles are delivered to them.

Upon our return to the United States, Peter and I were able to spend a day and a half in Hawaii. It had been a boyhood dream of mine to someday be able to visit the beautiful paradise of Hawaii. And now the Lord had made that dream a reality for me. The Lord truly does satisfy His children with good things.

23

"Go to Haiti and I will give you a miracle crusade!" These words repeatedly sounded in my ears. I had only been home from China for about two weeks when one evening while I was in prayer these words continued to come to my mind: "Go to Haiti and I will give you a miracle crusade."

I really didn't even know where Haiti was. As I began to meditate on these words, it became apparent to me that the Lord was leading me to go to Haiti and preach the Gospel. Finally I replied, "Okay Lord, just show me what to do, and I'll be glad to obey You!"

Several days went by and I received no direction from the Lord concerning Haiti so I began to dismiss the thought from my mind. Then one evening as I was attending a revival meeting at a local church, something was said that immediately arrested my attention. The guest speaker mentioned that he operated a mission station in Port au Prince, Haiti. Later that evening when the meeting had concluded, I introduced myself to Joe Mizell, the guest speaker.

Joe is the founder and president of an organization called World R.E.A.P. For Christ. The R.E.A.P. stands for Run Evangelize All People. Joe and I had coffee together and I shared with him what the Spirit of the Lord had spoken to me concerning Haiti. Joe listened intently. When I finished talking he said, "Dan, I believe the Lord wants me to help you. If you'll come to Haiti, you can stay at our mission house and we'll provide you with transportation and help set up some meetings for you in the local churches. I'll even see to it that you get an experienced interpreter to help you preach!"

"Well, Joe," I said, "I couldn't ask for anything more. I believe it's god's will, so let's start making the arrangements."

We prayed together and agreed that the first three weeks of April 1981 would be a good time for me to go to Haiti.

A few days later, I visited the Clarksburg Travel Agency

to reserve a round-trip plane ticket to Haiti. I didn't have any money at the time, but I did have the deep inner assurance that the Lord was leading me and that He would provide all of my needs. Later that week I attended a banquet meeting and one of the guest speakers there knew that I was making plans to go to Haiti. During the prayer time, this speaker requested that the congregation have a special prayer for me because I was planning to go to Haiti to preach the Gospel in April.

When the meeting had concluded, I went to a restaurant with some friends for a cup of coffee and some fellowship. After a waitress had taken our order, I happened to look, and I noticed that a couple was motioning for me to come over to their booth. They had been at the banquet meeting and heard that I was planning to go to Haiti in April.

"Well, Dan, have you purchased your airplane ticket and gotten everything ready to go to Haiti yet?" they asked.

"I reserved a seat on the airplane," I replied, "but I haven't paid for it yet."

"Do you think $700.00 would be enough to take care of your expenses?" they inquired.

"Well, yes," I said, "but ...

And before I could finish they said, "The Lord has impressed us to give you a check for $700.00 to help you with this trip."

"Well, praise the Lord, " I replied, "and God bless you for your obedience."

When I returned to my table and shared with my friends what the Lord had just done, we all rejoiced together. The Lord is so very good!

I arrived in Port au Prince, Haiti, around 9:00 p.m., Wednesday, April 1, 1981. Joe Mizell was there to meet me at the airport and transport me to the R.E.A.P. mission house. I picked up some literature and immediately began to learn a little about the history of Haiti.

Columbus discovered Haiti on December 5, 1492, two months after his first landfall at San Salvador and, later, Cuba. It was in 1697 that the authority of the French government was recognized in Haiti. On January 1, 1804, the independence of Haiti was proclaimed and the pecking order of black leadership was established. This order prevailed until 1957 when Dr. Francois ("Papa Doc") Duvalier was elected president. Later, in 1964 he would be elected President-for-Life, thus assuring himself and his successors a virtual dictatorship. From 1957 on, President-for-Life Duvalier withstood many conspiracies, armed attacks, mini-rebellions and hostile propaganda. But, according to the history books, even his detractors admit that the country with its 90 percent illiteracy rate needs a strong hand and a benevolent dictator. Before his death, Dr. Duvalier named his son, Jean-Claude Duvalier, President-for-Life. He assumed office on April 22, 1971.

Voodoo is practiced openly in Haiti and has been since its earliest history. It was a rain-swept night of violence on August 22, 1791, when voodoo worship became enthroned as the "official religion" of Haiti. The place was Morne Rouge, a mountain overlooking Cap Haitien. There, in the midst of the storm, Boukman, a voodoo priest, rallied his insurrectionists through a voodoo ceremony. The sacrificial pig was slain, the participants drank the warm blood, and the country was dedicated to the devil. The symbol of the white man's religion, the cross, was ripped off the necks of those present and trampled into the mud amid the frenzy of their dancing.

Voodoo is synonymous with the African word for "spirit." All voodooists know that there is a God, but there are so many *loa* or spirits to appease that one can never come to know Him. Christian holidays are also voodoo ceremonial days because these were the only days the slaves had free to practice their satanic rites. It was into this foreign, pagan society that I found myself thrust that April day in 1981.

I spent my first few days in Haiti getting acquainted with the people and the customs and preaching in several of the area churches. After some lengthy discussion with my interpreter, we came to the decision to drive back into the mountainous regions of the country and preach the Gospel there. We borrowed a four-wheel drive vehicle from the mission house and made the five-hour drive to a mountain village high above the city of Bainet on Haiti's southern coast. The devastation wrought by a recent killer storm was still apparent everywhere.

The drive to this mountain village was unbelievable. We drove for hours, bouncing endlessly over jagged rocks, and through a rushing stream with water coming up to the half-way mark on our doors. We drove to a point where driving was finally impossible and parked our vehicle, got out and walked the last half-hour to our final destination.

My interpreter and I spent the afternoon fellowshipping with the local natives and that evening we held a good old-time brush arbor meeting. My interpreter played an accordian and I spoke through a portable public address system. We attracted a crowd of over a hundred and fifty people that evening. Our only light was the full moon and one small candle. After preaching a simple salvation message, we witnessed several people dedicate their lives to Christ and others were miraculously healed of various diseases by the Lord. I was overjoyed to see the faithfulness of the Lord as several deaf people had their hearing restored after the prayer of faith was offered. The simple faith of these mountain villagers moved the mighty hand of God. Faith always pleases God and brings miraculous results.

I was thrilled by the results of my visit to Haiti, but as the time drew near for me to return to West Virginia, I began to question the Lord. "Lord," I said, "You told me that if I would come to Haiti, You would give me a miracle crusade. I truly thank You and praise You for the results we've experienced, but Lord, I was expecting something on a larger scale." As I continued to pray and meditate on the matter, I knew that the Lord wasn't finished yet.

Then, the day before I was to leave Haiti, I was put in touch with some people in Port au Prince who have a ministry of organizing crusades. They had recently worked together with R.E.A.P. in organizing a successful crusade for Evangelist R.W. Shaumbach with over 70,000 people in attendance. As I quietly sat and listened to them explain how they operate, faith rose in my heart and I said,

"Praise God, I'll do it! When can we begin to organize this crusade?"

We began to discuss preparations for the crusade, and it seemed good to the Holy Ghost and us to organize the cursade for the last week of June, 1981. That would give us about two months for all the preparations to be completed.

Upon returning home, I began to earnestly pray and seek the Lord as to how this step of faith I had taken would be financed. The cost of the crusade alone was a very reasonable $800.00. That would cover advertising, setting up a platform for an outdoor meeting, musicians and my interpreter. There would also be follow-up work done, but a majority of all the work would be done by volunteers. It would be a three-day crusade held in an open-air soccer field in the town of Jacmel. I was informed by the organizers to expect crowds of over 5,000 people each night. The meetings would be on Friday, Saturday and Sunday evenings, June 26, 27 and 28, 1981.

I knew in my heart that this was what the Lord wanted for me to do and as I prayed for His direction, the only response was, "Trust Me, son!" Then one morning as I was reading the Gospel of Matthew, my heart leaped within me as I read chapter fifteen, verses twenty-nine through thirty-one in the King James:

And Jesus departed from thence, and came nigh unto the sea of Galilee; and went up into a mountain and sat down there.

And great multitudes came unto him, having with them those that were lame, blind, dumb, maimed, and many others, and cast them down at Jesus' feet; and he healed them:

Insomuch that the multitude wondered, when they saw the dumb to speak, the maimed to be whole, the lame to walk, and the blind to see: and they glorified the God of Israel.

As I read these verses, the Spirit of the Lord spoke to me saying, "These same things will happen in your crusade in Jacmel!"

Then I continued to read: *Then Jesus called his disciples unto him, and said, I have compassion on the multitude, because they continue with me now three days, and have nothing to eat: and I will not send them away fasting, lest they faint in the way* (v. 32).

At this point I stopped reading and the Spirit of the Lord began to speak to me again: "I want you to feed the people at your crusade in Jacmel!"

As I sat and meditated on these words, my reply to the Lord was the same as the disciples' reply in verse 33: *And his disciples say unto him, Whence should we have so much bread in the wilderness as to fill so great a multitude?*

I knew from my past experience in Haiti that the majority of the people there live in poverty and many have very little if anything to eat. I was told to expect crowds of over 5,000 people each night. I didn't know how I would receive the $800.00 to pay for the crusade, and I didn't know yet how I was going to pay for my round-trip air fare to Haiti, plus my own personal expenses. Now, on top of all of this, the Lord was telling me to feed all the people at the crusade. My mind became flooded with doubts and fears, but surprisingly I had a calmness deep down in my heart.

As I finished reading the chapter, I saw that Jesus took what the disciples had, and performed a miracle with it. As I thought on that, I concluded that if Jesus Christ really is the same yesterday, today and forever, then He would do no less for me than He did for these disciples. How He would do it would be His business, but I needed nothing short of a miracle.

I continued in prayer and praise to God and shared my vision with my friends and wherever I was given the opportunity to preach. Then the miracle began to happen. On Wednesday evening, April 29, 1981, I was sitting in my car in Pennsboro, West Virginia. With me was a young man with whom I was earnestly counseling on the subject of the Bible experience of being baptized in the Holy Spirit and speaking with other tongues. As we concluded our conversation, the young man asked me if I would pray for him to receive the baptism in the Holy Spirit, and I agreed. As I laid my right hand upon his head I said, "Kelly, in the name of the Lord Jesus Christ, receive ye the Holy Ghost!" Immediately Kelly began to speak with other tongues as the Holy Spirit gave him utterance.

I have witnessed this same experience hundreds of

times, but it is always glorious and unique to the receiver. We rejoiced there together for quite some time. Then as Kelly was about to get out of my car, he handed me a one hundred dollar bill and said, "The Lord told me to give you this to help with your trip to Haiti."

"Thank you very much, Kelly," I replied, "and thank You too, Lord Jesus!"

I put the money in an envelope marked "Haiti Fund" and began to daily thank the Lord for supplying every need concerning this crusade. Four days later I received a check for $100.00 toward the crusade and the next day a check for $500.00 was mailed to me for the same purpose. Over a period of the next two weeks, various smaller amounts were given to me to be used for the crusade in Haiti. Then, exactly twenty days after that first one hundred dollar contribution, a concerned couple handed me a check for $1,000.00. Seven days after that, a lady came to me and said, "Dan, every time I pray and ask the Lord how much I should give toward your crusade in Haiti, I always receive the same answer, 'Everything!' So, here is a check that cleans out my entire savings account, and may God bless it." And she handed me her personal check for $716.71.

When the time arrived for me to depart for Haiti, I reviewed in amazement what had happened over the past 55 days. The Lord had sovereignly provided enough money for the crusade, including my air fare and all my personal expenses, plus enough money to buy rice and beans and meat to prepare a meal for well over five thousand people. Praise the Lord!

I left on a flight out of Pittsburgh on Wednesday, June 24, 1981. Accompanying me was a young Christian businessman from Uniontown, Pennsylvania, named Mike Allen. Mike and I were close friends and he had shared with me that even though he had been a Christian for several years, he had never personally witnessed a miracle of healing take place. He wanted to see for himself blind eyes opened and hearing restored to the deaf and crippled and lame people walking by the power of the Lord.

"Mike," I said, "the Lord has assured me that we will witness these miracles take place in this crusade."

We arrived in Port au Prince, Haiti, with great expectations. We spent the first two nights at the R.E.A.P. mission house and the next day we were driven to the village of Jacmel, where we checked into the lovely La Jacmelienne Beach Hotel.

Friday, June 26, 1981, was the first evening of the crusade. The air seemed to be charged with expectancy as I walked across the platform to the microphone. The platform was set in the open air at one end of a huge soccer field. The size of the field made the crowd look comparatively small even though there were well over three thousand people there. I took the microphone in my hand. The musicians had been playing and the people had been singing, dancing and praising the Lord for over an hour. They were ready to hear this white American evangelist talk to them about God. Mike and I, plus one other man, were the only white people there. That proved to be no problem whatsoever. The people were kind and loving and anxious to hear me speak.

This was a new experience for me, and I was trusting Jesus for every word. My interpreter was doing a remarkable job as together we presented the simple message of God's love to these needy people. Their response was equally remarkable. I gave an altar call for those who wanted to receive Jesus Christ as their personal Savior and Lord of their lives. Literally hundreds flooded the platform to confess their sins to God and accept His mercy and forgiveness. I was so overcome by the experiences that I forgot about praying for the sick. I spent most of Saturday relaxing and asking God for wisdom on how to handle the services that evening.

When we arrived at the soccer field, the crowd had more than doubled from Friday night. As the people clapped their hands and sang to the music, I walked around the huge field praying with other tongues asking the Lord to perform miracles on the sick and needy people there. As I continued to walk and pray, I heard the sound of voices behind me. Some of the children had left the crowd and were following me as I walked around the field. I stopped and waited for them to catch up with me. I felt like the pied piper as scores of children began to surround me. They had heard me praying and had come to investigate. Suddenly, I felt like a little child again. I couldn't speak their language, but I could communicate love to them. I began to skip and dance across the field like a carefree child. They all began to laugh and follow me, doing the same. For just a moment I felt like I knew a little of what heaven will be like. I savored the experience.

Moments later, I found myself back on the platform and preaching with great compassion about the healing power and love of Jesus Christ. I asked my interpreter to tell the people to bring their sick forward and I would pray for them and God would heal them. It was time to prove the Word of God. I prayed aloud and then one at a time they were brought to me. My interpreter would first ask each individual what his problem was. Then he would tell me and I would lay hands on that person and pray for his healing.

"This lady is blind," my interpreter said, "and she wants God to give her sight."

What could I do, but pray? Mike stood close by to witness the results.

"I command sight to be restored to these eyes in Jesus' name," I said boldly.

The lady looked at me for a moment. All was silent. I looked at my interpreter. He spoke to her and then she spoke to him in their native tongue. He smiled at me and said, "Praise God, Brother Nicholson, she said she is able to see you now!"

After this experience, I continued praying with great faith for every person who came forward. Several other blind people reported that their vision had been restored and a deaf man had his hearing restored after being prayed for.

A little girl was brought to me and the interpreter said, "She is over four years old and has never uttered a sound from her mouth." I picked her up and sat her in my lap. I placed my hand over her mouth and commanded, "Thou dumb spirit, in the name of Jesus Christ, come out of her and enter her no more!" She squealed loudly and tears began to flow down her mother's cheeks. In a moment she was repeating words as my interpreter spoke to her and the first word she repeated was the name Jesus.

Another mother came forward and pushed her child into my arms and began speaking frantically to me. I couldn't understand her and I looked at my interpreter and asked, "What is this all about?"

"Brother Nicholson," he replied, "this girl is over five years of age and she has never yet taken her first step. Her legs are like rubber and she falls down if they try to stand her up."

I held the little girl in my arms and prayed that her legs would receive strength to walk. I stood her upon her feet on the platform. With her hands in mine, she began walking across the platform into the arms of a grateful mother. The Lord was faithful in granting our requests.

The people were now pressing in on the platform from all directions. I called for Mike to come and help me pray for the sick and together we witnessed many miracles. Hours went by before we finally finished laying hands upon the sick and praying the prayer of faith. Mike had witnessed in abundance what he had hoped for, and we were both exhausted when the meeting came to a close. All we desired now was a good night's sleep.

We arose early the next morning to a hearty breakfast and then went to one of the local churches for a morning service. This was the day that we would be feeding the people and cooking had already begun early that morning. We had hundreds of pounds of beans and rice and we were able to purchase a beef and have it butchered there at the feeding grounds. We began feeding the people around 1:00 p.m., and the whole project seemed to get out of control. Starving people were coming at us from every direction holding out bowls, tin cans, cups, their hats or just anything that would hold a scoop of food.

"My God," I prayed, "how do we handle this situation?"

People continued pouring in all afternoon to be fed.

Many who hadn't eaten for days received a good hot meal that day. My thoughts went to the many generous people who had made this opportunity possible.

By evening, the crowd on the soccer field had almost doubled again. There was much excitement as the musicians encouraged the people to praise the Lord for His goodness. I introduced Mike to the people and he briefly addressed the crowd. I then began to preach to the people about God's love for them. That night hundreds more came to receive Jesus Christ as their Savior, and we once again prayed for the sick for several hours. The Lord was merciful and many received miraculous healings after being prayed for. The entire crusade was a testimony to me of what faith in God can really do. We must always remind ourselves and others that with God nothing shall be impossible.

24

The nature of my evangelistic work has been such that sometimes I have been very busy and other times I have had no meetings scheduled. During the times when I have not been busy, I have sometimes been tempted to wonder if maybe the Lord was through working with me. The thought has come to me that maybe nobody wants to hear what I have to share any more, that maybe I should just quit and find something else to do. We are all tempted at times to look at ourselves in a critical manner. You may be going through such an experience in your own life. But, friend, don't be too hard on yourself! Jesus Christ still loves you as you are. He is really with you there, right now. He has promised that He will never leave us nor forsake us. That promise has always been a comfort to me, and I believe that it is a comfort to you too. Remember, God is not a man that He should lie.

In my daily prayers I continue to ask God to use me for His glory and to open doors of opportunity for me that no man can close. There are so many hurting people around the world who need to hear the message that only Christians can give them, the Gospel message, the Good News message, the message of God's love for them.

In November 1981, the Lord performed another miracle which allowed me to visit the nation of Israel once again. I departed from New York City on November 14, 1981, to attend a Prophecy Conference in the city of Jerusalem led by Dr. Lester Sumrall. Since my first visit to Israel in January 1980, I have continued to pray for the peace of Jerusalem and for the salvation of the nation of Israel. I believe that every born-again Christian should be praying for Israel. We should make an attempt, by trusting God as our source, to visit the land where our Savior was born, crucified and resurrected, the land from which He ascended into heaven and to which He will soon return in glory.

When I went back to Israel for a second visit, I felt as if I were returning home. As our bus ascended the hill into the city of Jerusalem, I began to recall the words of Psalm 122 (*KJV*):

Our feet shall stand within thy gates, O Jerusalem.
Jerusalem is builded as a city that is compact together:
Wither the tribes go up, the tribes of the Lord, unto the testimony of Israel, to give thanks unto the name of the Lord.
For there are set thrones of judgment, the thrones of the house of David.
Pray for the peace of Jerusalem: they shall prosper that love thee.
Peace be within thy walls, and prosperity within thy palaces.
For my brethren and companions' sakes, I will now say, Peace be within thee.
Because of the house of the Lord our God I will seek thy good.

We stayed at the beautiful Jerusalem Hilton Hotel, where the Prophecy Conference was held on November 16, 17 and 18, with many inspiring speakers in attendance. During the conference I had the opportunity to talk with Dr. Sumrall about my deep desire to serve the Lord in a greater capacity. On Monday evening, Dr. Sumrall preached a very inspiring message and then invited to come forward for prayer all those who desired a greater anointing for service to the Lord. As Dr. Sumrall laid his hands upon my head and said, "Receive the anointing of the Lord!", I knew the power of the Holy Spirit was upon me for greater service.

The next night was a very special time for me. Everyone at the conference was captivated by the preaching and testimony of Pastor Buddy Harrison. When the meeting was dismissed, everyone retired to their rooms. I went to my room, but I wasn't at all sleepy. There was something in my heart that I wanted to do and I knew that I wouldn't be satisfied until I did it. I remembered reading in the Gospels that the garden of Gethsemane was a favorite place of Jesus'. Oftentimes He would retire to the Garden and spend the night in prayer.

I recalled my first visit to the Garden of Gethsemane two years earlier. I had knelt at the Rock of Agony to pray and had lifted my hands up toward heaven to praise the Lord. Then it had happened. It felt as if someone had taken a pitcher of warm honey and poured it down over my hands and arms, and the Spirit of the Lord had spoken to my heart, "Take My healing power to all nations." That experience is still very real to me. I also remembered how that since that experience, the Lord had miraculously given me the opportunity to travel to some eight different countries and witness many miracles of healing. I saw the blind receive sight, deaf ears opened, the crippled and lame walk, and the dumb speak by the power of God's anointing.

I grabbed a heavy coat from my closet and left my room around 10:30 p.m. As I walked outside the lobby of the hotel, and into the cool evening air, I looked around for a taxi cab. I spotted one.

"Sir, can you take me to the Mount of Olives tonight?" I asked.

"Five American dollars," was the reply.

"Let's go!"

The moon was bright and full as I stepped out of the cab and into the quietness and solitude of that place. I was just a few hundred feet from the historical spot where Jesus Christ ascended into heaven and to which He shall return according to the prophet Zechariah:

And his feet shall stand in that day upon the mount of Olives, which is before Jerusalem on the east, and the mount of Olives shall cleave in the midst thereof toward the east and toward the west, and there shall be a very great valley; and half of the mountain shall remove toward the north, and half of it toward the south.

Zechariah 14:4 KJV

As I walked slowly down the paved path that leads to the Kidron Valley, I remembered how at one time Jesus rode a colt down this path:

And many spread their garments in the way: and others cut down branches off the trees, and strawed them in the way.

And they that went before, and they that followed, cried, saying, Hosanna; Blessed is he that cometh in the name of the Lord.

Blessed be the kingdom of our father David, that cometh in the name of the Lord: Hosanna in the highest.

Mark 11:8-10 KJV

As I walked, I began to pray and make intercession in the Spirit. It was around 11:00 p.m. when I walked into the Garden of Gethsemane and knelt beside an olive tree to pray. There was such a sweet serenity in that time of prayer as the hours slipped away. I sensed the presence of the Lord as I prayed for so many people and situations that were heavy upon my heart. I knew that there was victory in every petition. I prayed and waited for the Lord to speak to my heart. And in that time of waiting, He spoke only three words to me. They were mighty words indeed: "Heal My people!"

The words echoed over and over again in my spirit and in my head: "Heal My people!" I could see it now. I received a blessed peace in my heart and I began to understand. God really does want His people to be in health and to prosper, even as their souls prosper. (3 John 2.) The tears streamed down my face as I cried to the Lord, "Jesus, help me to heal Your people."

Everything grew calm and peaceful. It began to rain ever so gently. It was around 5:00 a.m. and I could hear the Moslems' prayers being offered across the golden Dome on the Rock silhouetted against the gray morning sky. At that moment I knew that God loved the Moslems, the Jews, the Arabs, the Christians, the Gentiles and all people everywhere. The heart cry of God is for all people, everywhere, to be healed, to be saved, to be free. "Heal My people!" He says. He alone has that healing balm of Gilead. It cannot be found in Mohammad or the Law of Moses or in money or in church membership or in great works of humanitarianism. It can only come through a humble admission that we are all helpless in ourselves, and through an acceptance of His grace—freely given to all people, everywhere, through faith expressed in Jesus Christ, the only true Savior of the world.

Jesus Christ has changed my life from hippie to happy. I don't know exactly what the Lord has in store for me next, but whatever it may be, I know I'll be happy to do it. My happiness no longer depends upon who, what or where. I have discovered that true happiness is living daily with Jesus. I have learned to be content in whatever circumstances I find myself, because I know that He is working everything together for my ultimate good.

You too can be continually happy, if you will simply begin right now to practice Proverbs 3:5-6:

Trust in the Lord with all your heart, and do not lean on your own understanding.

In all your ways acknowledge Him and He will make your paths straight.

Remember: *Happy is that people, whose God is the Lord* (Ps. 144:15b *KJV*).

Epilogue

Thou wilt shew me the path of life: in thy presence is fulness of joy; at thy right hand there are pleasures for evermore.
Psalm 16:11 KJV

On November 14, 1980, I had a lengthy conversation with David du Plessis in which he told me that the New Testament Christians should not be compared to a flock of sheep. Sheep are animals that do not care for one another, and they are constantly going astray.

In 2 Corinthians 12:12-31 the Apostle Paul compares us to a body, not a flock. In verse 27 he writes: *Now you are Christ's body, and individually members of it.* Jesus Christ is the head of this body and, if we are truly born again, then we are all individual members of that body, sharing and caring for one another. Our only commandment in the New Testament is the one Jesus gave us in the Gospel of John, chapter thirteen, verses thirty-four and thirty-five:

"A new commandment I give to you, that you love one another, even as I have loved you, that you also love one another."

"By this all men will know that you are My disciples, if you have love for one another."

"If" can be a mighty big word. *If* we love one another, THEN the world will know Him. And if we don't, they won't. Jesus didn't *ask* us to love one another, He *commanded* us to do so. And He said that if we really loved Him, then we would keep His commandment.

Love really can be contagious, and I believe it's time for us to have an epidemic of the Jesus kind of love. Certainly, all churches and Christians will not agree on everything. But we must still love and care for one another, if the world is ever going to know Jesus.

Remember, it's not so much our responsibility as it is our response to His ability. He lives in us by faith, and He is able. God is not asking about our ability, but He is asking about our availability. If we will make ourselves available to the Lord on a daily basis, then we will live in true happiness.

Let's leave the judging of other people's lives to God,

and let's begin to act like a real body and not a flock. A real body will always fight to heal itself and not to amputate its own members. With God nothing shall be impossible. If we expect to receive God's unconditional love in our own lives, then we must be willing to demonstrate that unconditional love toward one another.

If you've enjoyed reading this true episode of my search and seizure of true happiness, then please take a moment just now to look toward heaven and ask our Heavenly Father to bless this book. Ask Him to use it to spread true happiness around the world and to continue to guide my life daily in His happy plans, in Jesus' name. Thank you!

If you forget everything else, please remember this: Jesus loves you. He really does care about your life right now, and He wants to make you happy — right now! There really is no other way! Make your decision, and be happy today.

Whosoever trusteth in the Lord, happy is he.
Proverbs 16:20 KJV

Having many things to write to you, I do not want to do so with paper and ink; but I hope to come to you and speak face to face, that our joy may be made full.
2 John 12

ABOUT THE AUTHOR

Dan Nicholson and his wife Betsy were married on April 24, 1982. At present they are the pastors of Indian Lake Christian Center, an independent, Full-Gospel fellowship near Central City, Pennsylvania. They also serve as principals of Indian Lake Christian Academy, a Christian school for grades K-12. In addition, they lead an annual group tour of the Holy Land to help Christians to gain a deeper understanding of the Scriptures and to experience a renewed spiritual commitment.

Since November 1981, Dan has been a frequent host and co-host for Russ Bixler's "Getting Together" program on WPCB TV-40 near Pittsburg, Pennsylvania.

For information concerning speaking engagements, tapes or travel, please contact:

Daniel A. Nicholson
P.O. Box 121
Central City, PA. 15926
Phone: (814) 267-3535